# Hygiene and Related Behaviors for Children and Adolescents with Autism Spectrum and Related Disorders

## A Fun Curriculum with a Focus on Social Understanding

Kelly J. Mahler, MS, OTR/L

# APC

Autism Asperger Publishing Co.
P.O. Box 23173
Shawnee Mission, Kansas 66283-0173
www.asperger.net

© 2009 AAPC
P.O. Box 23173
Shawnee Mission, Kansas 66283-0173
www.asperger.net · 913.897.1004

Publisher's Cataloging-in-Publication

Mahler, Kelly J.
    Hygiene and related behaviors for children and adolescents with autism spectrum and related disorders : a fun curriculum with a focus on social understanding / Kelly J. Mahler. -- 1st ed. -- Shawnee Mission, Kan. : Autism Asperger Pub. Co., c2009.
        p. ; cm.
        ISBN: 978-1-934575-42-0
        Includes bibliographical references.
        LCCN: 2009923883

    1. Autistic children--Health and hygiene. 2. Autistic youth--Health and hygiene. 3. Social skills in children--Study and teaching. 4. Social skills in adolescence--Study and teaching. I. Title.

RJ506.A9 M34 2009
618.92/858832--dc22                                        0904

This book is designed in Helvetica Neue.

Printed in the United States of America.

# Table of Contents

**Introduction**

# An Overview and Introduction to the Curriculum

# What You Can Expect

*Hygiene and Related Behaviors for Children and Adolescents with Autism Spectrum and Related Disorders* teaches important hygiene skills and associated social understanding concepts in a fun, yet structured manner. The curriculum is aimed at meeting the constant search for inventive and intriguing methods for teaching often quite boring topics surrounding functional life skills.

Over the years, I have found that, although participants were laughing and having fun, they were improving their skills. What better way to teach and learn.

## Success Stories

- **Clay, 10th grader** – *Clay detested showering. Every night, a battle between Clay and his parents would erupt surrounding the issue. Typically, Clay would win out, and another day would pass without him taking a shower. On average, Clay was showering twice a week. As a result, he often arrived at school with greasy hair, dirty skin and fingernails – and a very ripe odor.*

  *At school, Clay desperately wanted to fit in and make friends. Additionally, he had developed his first serious crush on a girl and wanted to talk to her at lunch. But due to his poor hygiene, everyone avoided Clay.*

  *For years, his parents and teachers had emphasized to Clay how important hygiene is, how "everyone showers every day," etc., but it wasn't until Clay started receiving instruction using the activities in this book that changes started occurring. The visual, structured nature of the activities helped Clay see the powerful impact that his hygiene, or lack thereof, was having on his ability to fit in socially. Additionally, because the activities were fun, Clay finally relaxed and was more open about this topic that had caused him and his family years of tension. Using laughter, Clay lowered his guard and was able to learn the skills necessary. After a few lessons, Clay started showering on his own every night!*

- **Lizzie, 7ᵗʰ grader** – *Lizzie had a very limited repertoire of clothing that she was willing to wear to school. In fact, she had exactly two pairs of sweatpants and two t-shirts that she would wear, alternating them across the days of the week. Although Lizzie's outfits had quite a few stains and tears, she refused to wear anything different. In addition to the unclean appearance of her clothes, the type of pants she chose to wear were not exactly what the other seventh-grade girls were wearing.*

  *Lizzie's supportive mother was exhausted from her unsuccessful attempts at expanding Lizzie's wardrobe to contain a few clean, comfortable, and "peer-acceptable" pieces, and had pretty much given up.*

  *To help remedy the situation, Lizzie's occupational therapist, speech-language pathologist, teacher, and mother worked together, using many of the lessons from this curriculum. The structured nature of the lessons and activities helped Lizzie understand that her appearance was impacting her ability to fit in and make friends. Lizzie was amazed to learn that her appearance, specifically her clothing, affected the way others were thinking and feeling about her.*

  *Once she understood these concepts, she was motivated to expand her wardrobe. Through a lot of trial and error, and a lot of courage on Lizzie's part, she was able to find a brand of jeans that were comfortable for her to wear. She also allowed her mother to buy her a few new t-shirts.*

## What Makes This Curriculum Effective?

Good hygiene is an important aspect of our social world, as personal hygiene habits directly impact not only our health but also the thoughts and feelings of people around us. Children and youth are typically taught to shower every day or wear clean clothes to school, but often are not told "why" as we assume that is a given – others like us to be clean and well-groomed without bad breath and unpleasant body odor.

But many individuals with autism spectrum disorders (ASD) have deficits in perspective taking (Attwood, 2007; Winner, 2002) and do not naturally link personal hygiene habits to their ability to make good impressions on others. Further, there are many unwritten "social rules" surrounding hygiene and related behaviors. These social rules, often referred to as the "hidden curriculum" (Myles, Trautman, & Schelvan, 2004), are frequently assumed to be known by all. However, individuals with ASD typically fail to learn these rules intuitively. This curriculum provides an avenue for learning those unwritten social rules and why they are important to social success.

When working on hygiene skills with this group of students, therefore, it is important to teach both *how* to have good hygiene and *why* it is important, and to do so in a concrete and meaningful manner that maximizes their learning styles. This curriculum acknowledges the unique learning needs of individuals with ASD and teaches the "how-tos" and "whys" of hygiene in a very concrete manner. Therefore, a heavy emphasis is placed on appealing to their visual strengths (Attwood, 2007). For example, the instructional materials and supports that are part of each lesson help to enhance the correlating activity or game in a visual manner. In addition, after the lesson is completed, the instructional materials can serve as visual reminders of the skill learned, helping students to generalize the skill to everyday life.

## Who Will Benefit from This Curriculum?

*Hygiene and Related Behaviors for Children and Adolescents with Autism Spectrum and Related Disorders* targets the skills needed by many children, adolescents, and teenagers with high-functioning autism (HFA), Asperger Syndrome (AS), and related diagnoses.

## Who Can Teach This Curriculum?

This book was developed for those who are searching for a fun, creative, and easy way to teach the crucial life skills related to hygiene. *Hygiene and Related Behaviors for Children and Adolescents with Autism Spectrum and Related Disorders* can be implemented by a variety of professionals, including teachers, occupational therapists, speech-language pathologists, social workers, and psychologists. Additionally, the curriculum can be easily used by parents in the comfort of their own home.

Finally, the accompanying CD includes all worksheets and activity materials to make planning and implementation easier and less time-consuming.

## Chapter 1

# Getting Started

# Using the Curriculum

This curriculum is designed to be flexible so it can be put to use without major preparation by professionals or parents working on hygiene issues with children and adolescents with autism spectrum or related disorders.

Each chapter provides a set of suggested lesson plans. They may be used as presented or be adapted to meet the needs of the individuals with whom you are working. Each lesson plan, comprised of various activities and instructional materials, is designed to take approximately 45 minutes to complete. If this length of time is not available, or if you wish to tailor instruction to individual needs, you can forego the lesson plans and instead select from the menu of activities and instructional materials provided in each chapter. The length of time needed for each activity varies, ranging from 5 to 30 minutes.

Each chapter contains the following four components:

## Objectives

- The objective statement lists the main focus of each individual chapter.

## Lesson Plans

- The suggested lesson plans outline complete instructional sessions, infusing all of the activities and instructional materials listed in each chapter in a systematic and structured manner. The suggested lesson plans are described in greater detail later in this chapter.

## Activities

- The suggested activities provide fun and creative ideas for teaching important hygiene topics and the related perspective-taking skills.
- Each activity is explained in detail, including a sequential description of instructions and a list of materials needed to complete the activity.
- The activities for a particular topic are listed at the beginning of each chapter.

## Instructional Materials and Supports

- The instructional materials and supports are designed to support individual activities. Additionally, a variety of supports are provided to encourage carryover and generalization of hygiene and perspective-taking skills to real-life situations.
- Each support is provided in a reproducible format.
- The supports for a particular topic are listed at the beginning of each chapter.

# Selecting Participants

The curriculum was designed to target a wide range of individuals with HFA, AS, and related diagnoses. It can be used with a single participant or with a group.

With simple adjustments, such as altering the length of the activity, the curriculum can be used with young children in addition to older children and adolescents. Certain aspects of the curriculum have been helpful for adults (e.g., responding to farting/burping behaviors).

---

### Perspective Taking

When selecting participants, please consider a few prerequisite perspective-taking skills. While developing perspective-taking skills is a large focus of this curriculum, it is helpful for the participant to have some basic understanding of common perspective-taking concepts such as those mentioned by Winner (2002). For example, they should understand that other people have thoughts different from their own. They should also understand that their behaviors can impact others' thoughts and feelings. Please refer to the section Creating a Foundation for Perspective-Taking Skills on page 11 for further details

---

# Using a Group Format

As mentioned, the contents of this book can be used with an individual participant as well as a group of participants. If using a group format, keep the following in mind:

## Ages

- Topics surrounding hygiene vary as a person matures. Therefore, it is helpful to join individuals of similar age or developmental level. Maintaining a small range of ages or skills will allow for the most accurate and detailed instruction.

## Number of Participants

- When determining the size of the group, consider candidates' age, ability level, and maturity. The higher their level of independence, the more participants can be included and still function successfully in the group. Suggested group size ranges from 2-10 participants.

## Location of Group

- The curriculum is designed to be implemented in a variety of environments, including a school, a clinic, or home. It is helpful to have access to a sink or full bathroom to complete some of the activities.

# General Format of Lesson Plans

The suggested lesson plans in each chapter follow an-easy-to-use format. They are provided as examples of how to combine the activities and instructional materials in a systematic way, but they do not need to be followed precisely in order for the curriculum to be effective. You can disregard the lesson plans as presented and choose from the menu of activities provided in each chapter if that better meets the needs of your participant/group.

Each lesson plan contains four main components: an outline of the session schedule, the details of the lesson, the materials needed to complete the session, and a list of items to add to the binders (see page 9) following the lesson.

## Session Schedule

- The session schedule, listed at the top of each lesson plan, is a brief overview of the activities included. It is strongly recommended that you post this schedule in a place where all participants can easily refer to it for a visual support. Providing the schedule in writing not only allows participants to know what to anticipate, it also gives a clear list of what is expected of each participant (e.g., completion of each activity) as well as a clear ending point to the lesson.

## Lesson Details

- The lesson details section provides a sequential list of activities to use during the lesson.
- Each lesson takes approximately 45 minutes. The estimated time needed for individual activities is listed in the "Estimated Time" column.
- Only the title of each activity is provided on the lesson plan page. For a full description of activities, refer to the page listed in the column next to each corresponding item.

## Needed Materials

- The needed materials section contains a checklist of all items necessary to carry out a given lesson plan.

# Binders

It is recommended that participants create a binder or folder to organize all instructional materials and supports. The binder may be divided into sections according to skill topics (Oral Hygiene, Bathroom Hygiene, etc.).

- *Use the binder for review and generalization.* Following each lesson, encourage participants to file the materials provided in the corresponding section. When reviewing skills or generalizing skills to real life, it is helpful to have the instructional materials and supports easily accessible in the organized binder.
- *Use the binder to maintain a home-school communication.* If instruction is occurring in a school or clinic, communication between home and school/clinic is an important part of the curriculum. When possible, recruiting all members of the child's team for support typically increases the success that the child will experience. The binder can serve as a useful tool in relaying information and resources back and forth between environments. Additionally, creating a binder for each environment allows the child easy access to the support materials.

# Using a Consistent Lesson Design

Each lesson plan follows a similar format to provide participants with a sense of consistency and predictability, which can alleviate anxiety (Attwood, 2007) – a common concern among students with ASD and similar disorders. It is recommended that each lesson be led by consistently using the following design.

## Welcome and Introduction

- Posting and review of schedule – Prior to the start of the lesson, briefly review the schedule posted with participants. Use positive terminology and create a sense of excitement. For example, if doing an activity, write "Fun Activity," "Special Activity," or "Surprise!!" on the schedule. These descriptive words have positive connotations and set the stage for an upbeat lesson. For convenience, each lesson plan contains a sample schedule that can be given to the participants, incorporating these positive descriptors. Here is an example of a schedule:

    1. Chat and review
    2. Fun activity
    3. Game
    4. Surprise (if earned)
    5. Closing

## Instruction

- Discussion of topic
- Fun activity(ies)

## Closing

- Reward – At times it is helpful to motivate participants with a concrete reward if a specific goal is met. At the beginning of the lesson, clearly state or write the goal for the lesson, providing participants with a specific target. At the end of the session, if the participants meet the goal, provide a reward such as a healthy snack, a fun game, or short movie clip.

# Creating a Foundation for Perspective-Taking Skills

As mentioned, the curriculum will be most successful if participants have a basic foundation of perspective-taking skills. In the simplest of terms, perspective-taking skills refer to the ability to recognize and understand one's own thoughts and feelings, as well as the thoughts and feelings of others (Winner, 2002).

Effective perspective taking is essential for maintaining socially appropriate hygiene and related behaviors. Many of us learn early on that our hygiene directly impacts the thoughts and feelings of others. We learned to follow the unwritten social rules (a.k.a. hidden curriculum) of hygiene in order to make a positive impression on others. Thus, maintaining this positive impression became our motivation for maintaining good hygiene even on the days when we did not feel like showering or brushing our teeth. If we were unable to understand how our hygiene habits impact others' thoughts and feelings, would we maintain such a high quality of hygiene all of the time? Honestly, probably not!

Impaired perspective taking is a core deficit of individuals with ASD (Baron-Cohen, Leslie, & Frith, 1985). Many need to be taught perspective-taking skills through systematic instruction and practice. As part of this learning process, specific focus should be placed on the area of hygiene and related behaviors. Many individuals with ASD never consider that their hygiene, or lack thereof, has a direct impact on how others think and feel about them. This curriculum will explore this notion in detail while enhancing each participant's perspective-taking skills.

A comprehensive discussion of how to build perspective taking is beyond the bounds of this curriculum. However, there are several helpful resources on this and related topics, including the following:

- *Building Social Relationships* by Scott Bellini
- *Think Social! A Social Thinking Curriculum for School-Aged Students* by Michelle G. Winner
- *Thinking About You, Thinking About Me* by Michelle G. Winner
- *Comic Strip Conversations* by Carol Gray

(See References for complete information.)

# The Unwritten Social Rules Related to Hygiene

There are many unwritten social rules surrounding hygiene and related behaviors. Following these rules, often referred to as the hidden curriculum (Myles et al., 2004), is crucial to achieving social success and maintaining health and safety. Typically, these rules are innately learned. However, many individuals with ASD do not automatically learn them. Not knowing or understanding the hidden curriculum items covered in this book can lead to social disaster or in some cases may lead to very unsafe situations.

In order to improve the social success experienced by participants, these unwritten social rules need to be concretely explained and practiced. This book serves as a guide for teaching many hidden curriculum items surrounding hygiene and related behaviors. However, because these rules are extremely complex and depend on factors such as age, gender, culture, and environment (Myles et al., 2004), the book does not claim to cover *all* items of the hidden curriculum related to hygiene. Rather, it is intended to serve as a guide in discovering ways to teach these hidden social rules and *why* they are so important. It may be necessary to change the rules provided so that they are more appropriate for the participant's age, gender, culture, etc. Additionally, it may be necessary to add rules to the existing material. This is strongly encouraged to ensure the best possible results.

# Self-Regulation

While an in-depth discussion of self-regulation is beyond the scope of this book, it is important to briefly mention the importance of self-regulation. Having basic self-regulation skills is essential to the success of this program as well as success in life in general. Most individuals with ASD have impaired self-regulation abilities (Attwood, 2007). Their impairments fall into three main domains:

- Sensory Regulation
- Energy Regulation
- Emotional Regulation

Individuals may have deficits in one or all of these domains. In order for them to become effective and independent self-regulators, comprehensive, systematic instruction must be provided. Part of this instruction should focus on generalization of the learned skills to real-life situations (Attwood, 2007).

In order to promote practice and carryover of learned self-regulation skills, it may be helpful to remind participants to "check" their minds and bodies prior to the start of each lesson (Buron &

Curtis, 2003). Also encourage participants to use tools that will allow for their bodies to reach an optimal level for learning prior to the start of an activity/lesson (e.g., a quiet break, music, a walk) or the use of tools during the activity/lesson (e.g., hand fidgets, mouth fidgets, behavior checklist).

For assistance regarding development of self-regulation skills in students, including sensory regulation, energy regulation, and emotional regulation, consult an occupational therapist.

Additionally, several helpful resources address self-regulation and related topics for students with ASD, including the following:

- *The Incredible 5-point Scale* by Kari Dunn Buron and Mitzi Curtis
- *Exploring Feelings: Cognitive Behavior Therapy to Manage Anxiety* by Tony Attwood
- *Asperger Syndrome and Difficult Moments: Practical Solutions for Tantrums, Rage, and Meltdowns* by Brenda Smith Myles and Jack Southwick
- *A "Five" Could Make Me Lose Control* by Kari Dunn Buron
- *My Sensory Book: Working Together to Explore Sensory Issues and the Big Feelings They Can Cause: A Workbook for Parents, Professionals, and Children* by Lauren Kerstein
- *Exploring Feelings: Cognitive Behavior Therapy to Manage Anger* by Tony Attwood
- *The Alert Program* by Mary Sue Williams and Sherry Shellenberger

# Chapter 2

# Introduction to Good Hygiene

---

## **Chapter Objectives:**

- To establish basic knowledge of good hygiene practices.
- To understand the connection between personal hygiene and the thoughts and feelings of others.
- To understand the unwritten social rules surrounding hygiene.

---

# List of Activities

The following is a list of activities in this chapter. Please refer to the subsequent pages for a complete description of each.

1. Introduction to Good Hygiene – Questions

2. Introduction to Good Hygiene – Discussion Guide

3. I Can Read Your Mind

4. My Hygiene Routine

5. Search and Find and Read Your Mind

6. Hygiene Poster

7. Every Vote Counts

8. Hygiene Competition

9. Hygiene Wrap-Up

# List of Instructional Materials and Supports

The following is a list of instructional materials and supports that can be used to enhance the activities and lessons in this chapter. Please refer to the subsequent pages for a copy of each.

1. Introduction to Good Hygiene – Questions

2. Introduction to Good Hygiene – Discussion Guide

3. Hygiene Thought Bubble Worksheet

4. My Morning Hygiene Routine

5. My Evening Hygiene Routine

6. Sample Morning Hygiene Routine

7. Sample Evening Hygiene Routine

8. Hygiene Thought Bubble Worksheet – Homework Version

9. Hygiene Voting Cards

10. Sample Hygiene Rating Form

11. Hygiene Rating Form

12. Hygiene Wrap-Up Questions

# Introduction to Good Hygiene – Lesson Plan 1

## Session Schedule to Post:

- Chat – introduction to good hygiene
- Fun activity
- Closing (snack, reward, etc.)

## Lesson Details:

| Estimated Time | Activity | Refer to Pages: |
|---|---|---|
| 5 minutes | Opening – Gather participants. Post and review schedule for session | |
| 10 minutes | Hygiene Activity #1 –"Introduction to Good Hygiene – Questions" | 19-20 |
| 10 minutes | Hygiene Activity #2 – "Introduction to Good Hygiene – Discussion Guide" to facilitate further discussion and provide any missed information | 21-23 |
| 15 minutes | Hygiene Activity #3 – "I Can Read Your Mind" | 24-25 |
| 5 minutes | Closing | |

## Needed Materials:

☐ Instructional Materials and Supports:

"Introduction to Good Hygiene – Questions" (1 copy per participant)

"Introduction to Good Hygiene – Discussion Guide" (1 copy per participant)

"Hygiene Thought Bubble Worksheet" (2 copies per participant)

☐ Pictures of people with good and poor hygiene. Please refer to References and Other Resources for tips on finding pictures (2 pictures per participant)

☐ Pencils

☐ Scissors

☐ Glue

☐ Binders

## Following Session, Add to Binder:

"Introduction to Good Hygiene – Questions" – completed version

"Introduction to Good Hygiene – Discussion Guide"

"Hygiene Thought Bubble Worksheets" – completed version

# Hygiene Activity #1
# "Introduction to Good Hygiene – Questions"

## Instructions:

|  | 1. | Give participants a copy of "Introduction to Good Hygiene – Questions." |
|---|---|---|
|  | 2. | Instruct participants to write answers to the questions on their worksheet. If writing is a source of anxiety or frustration, offer accommodations (i.e., scribe partner with another participant, etc.). |
|  | 3. | Set timer for a designated time period (approximately 5 minutes), if needed. |
|  | 4. | When participants are finished, read the first question aloud to the group. |
|  | 5. | Have participants share their answer. Discuss. |
|  | 6. | Repeat Steps 4-5 until each question has been is discussed. |

## Needed Materials:

☐ Instructional Materials and Supports:

"Introduction to Good Hygiene - Questions" (1 copy per participant)

☐ Pencils

☐ Binders

☐ Introduction to Good Hygiene – Lesson Plan 1

# Introduction to Good Hygiene – Questions

**Instructions:** After reading the question, write your answer in the space provided.

What does "good hygiene" mean?

How do hygiene habits impact the thoughts and feelings of other people?

What tasks should I do to have good hygiene?

1.

2.

3.

4.

5.

6.

7.

8.

What hygiene products should I have available?

What are some potential health problems that could arise as a result of poor hygiene?

# Hygiene Activity #2
# "Introduction to Good Hygiene – Discussion Guide"

## Instructions:

|  | |
|---|---|
|  | 1. Give each participant a copy of "Introduction to Good Hygiene – Discussion Guide." |
|  | 2. Read the first question aloud. |
|  | 3. Choose a participant to answer the question by reading the information provided on the worksheet or by expanding on the information on the worksheet. |
|  | 4. Challenge the other participants to think of additional information that is not provided on the worksheet. |
|  | 5. Repeat Steps 2-4 until all of the questions have been discussed. |

## Needed Materials:

☐ Instructional Materials and Supports:

"Introduction to Good Hygiene – Discussion Guide" (1 copy per participant)

☐ Pencils

☐ Binders

☐ Introduction to Good Hygiene – Lesson Plan 1

# Introduction to Good Hygiene – Discussion Guide

## What does "good hygiene" mean?

Keeping yourself looking neat and clean.

## How do good hygiene habits impact the thoughts and feelings of other people?

It helps you make a good impression on others. Having good hygiene will give others "good" thoughts about you. Having poor hygiene will give others "weird" or "gross" thoughts about you.

## What tasks should I do to have good hygiene?

It is important to follow a hygiene routine every day that helps you stay neat and clean. Everyone's hygiene routine is different, but here are a few important things to think about.

1. **Shower every day**
   - wash your entire body with soap; important areas to wash thoroughly include armpits, feet, face, and genital area
   - wash your hair with shampoo

2. **Comb your hair every morning**
   - make sure that your hair is not "sticking up"

3. **Clean your finger nails**
   - keep your nails short by cutting them with nail clippers every 2 weeks
   - remove dirt from under your nails with a nail brush

4. **Use deodorant**
   - apply deodorant every morning
   - may also apply deodorant before vigorous activities

5. **Dress nicely**
   - always wear clean clothes that don't have a foul odor

## 6. Brush your teeth

- brush your teeth at least 2 times a day (one time in the morning and one time in the afternoon)

## 7. Do frequent checks throughout the day (try to find a mirror)

- check your face for dirt and food
- check your teeth for food
- check your clothes for dirt and food
- check your hair to be sure it doesn't stick up

## What hygiene products should you have available?

- Shampoo
- Soap
- Deodorant
- Toothbrush
- Toothpaste
- Nail clippers
- Hair comb or brush

## What are some potential health problems that could arise as a result of poor hygiene?

- Develop infections (e.g., fungal infections of skin)
- Develop tooth decay and lose teeth
- Long fingernails can house a variety of bacteria and fungus that can make you sick (for example, when you are eating, the bacteria from under your long fingernails can transfer to the food and then transfer to your mouth)

# Hygiene Activity #3
# "I Can Read Your Mind"

## Instructions:

|  |  |
|---|---|
|  | 1. Give each participant 2 pictures of people demonstrating good and poor hygiene habits. |
|  | 2. Have participants cut and glue the first picture on a "Hygiene Thought Bubble Worksheet." |
|  | 3. Instruct participants to begin completing the first "Hygiene Thought Bubble worksheet" by determining if the picture is an example of socially O.K. hygiene or socially inappropriate hygiene. |
|  | 4. To complete the first worksheet, encourage participants to list the common thoughts and feelings the other person would have, based on the hygiene of the person in the picture. Have them write their answers in the blank thought bubble provided. You may need to support participants if they are having difficulty. For example, you can write a list of potential thoughts and feelings on the board and have participants select from the list (to add difficulty, provide some correct answers and some answers that are incorrect). |
|  | 5. To complete the assignment, instruct participants to repeat Steps 2-4 using the second picture. |
|  | 6. When everyone is finished, have each participant share the end product with the group. |

## Needed Materials:

☐ Instructional Materials and Supports:

"Hygiene Thought Bubble Worksheet" (2 copies per participant)

☐ Pictures of people with good and poor hygiene – include pictures of people with well-groomed hair, dirty or messy hair, clean nails, long and dirty nails, dirty clothes, clean clothes, dirty face, clean face, gross teeth, etc. Please refer to References and Other Resources for tips on finding pictures (2 pictures per participant)

☐ Pencils

☐ Scissors

☐ Glue

☐ Binders

☐ Introduction to Good Hygiene – Lesson Plan 1

# Hygiene Thought Bubble Worksheet

## Instructions:

1. Attach a picture in the designated area.
2. Determine if the person in the picture demonstrates socially O.K. hygiene or socially inappropriate hygiene by circling the corresponding answer in the area below.
3. Based on the hygiene of the person in the picture, list the common thoughts and feelings the other person might have in the blank thought bubble provided.

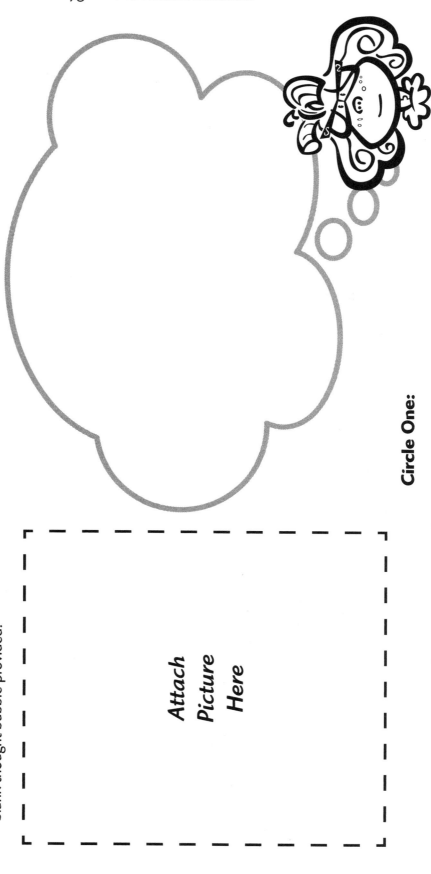

**Circle One:**

Socially O.K. Hygiene                Socially Inappropriate Hygiene

Attach Picture Here

# Introduction to Good Hygiene – Lesson Plan 2

## Session Schedule to Post:

- Chat and review
- Create hygiene routine
- Special assignment
- Closing (snack, reward, etc.)

## Lesson Details:

| Estimated Time | Activity | Refer to Pages: |
|---|---|---|
| 5 minutes | Opening – Gather participants. Post and review schedule for session | |
| 5 minutes | REVIEW – Have participants briefly recall the information covered in the previous session. If needed, refer them to the following forms added to their binders: "Introduction to Good Hygiene – Questions" and "Introduction to Good Hygiene – Discussion Guide" | |
| 25 minutes | Hygiene Activity #4 – "My Hygiene Routine" | 27-31 |
| 5 minutes | Assign and Explain Hygiene Activity #5 – "Search and Find and Read Your Mind" – DUE next group session | 32-33 |
| 5 minutes | Closing | |

## Needed Materials:

- ☐ Instructional Materials and Supports:
  "My Morning Hygiene Routine" (1 copy per participant)
  "My Evening Hygiene Routine" (1 copy per participant)
  "Sample Morning Hygiene Routine" (1 copy per participant)
  "Sample Evening Hygiene Routine" (1 copy per participant)
  "Hygiene Thought Bubble Worksheet – Homework Version" (2 copies per participant)
- ☐ Pencils
- ☐ Markers
- ☐ Wipe board or large piece of paper
- ☐ Binders

## Following Session, Add to Binder:

- ☐ "My Morning Hygiene Routine" – completed version
- ☐ "My Evening Hygiene Routine" – completed version
- ☐ "Morning Hygiene Routine – Sample Page"
- ☐ "Evening Hygiene Routine – Sample Page"

# Hygiene Activity #4
# "My Hygiene Routine"

## Instructions:

| | |
|---|---|
| | 1. Using input from participants, generate a list on the board or a large piece of paper of all tasks important for maintaining good hygiene. If needed, refer participants to "Introduction to Good Hygiene – Discussion Guide" (used during Hygiene Activity #2). |
| | 2. Give each participant a copy of:<br>• "My Morning Hygiene Routine"<br>• "My Evening Hygiene Routine"<br>• "Sample Morning Hygiene Routine"<br>• "Sample Evening Hygiene Routine" |
| | 3. Lead a discussion about hygiene routines, explaining that most people develop a consistent routine or hygiene schedule that allows them to complete necessary tasks in a time-efficient and organized manner. Also, following a consistent routine can ensure that an important task or tasks needed for good hygiene are not missed. Discuss the importance of this routine and ask participants to briefly share their routines with the group. |
| | 4. Review the sample routine outlined on "Sample Morning Hygiene Routine" and "Sample Evening Hygiene Routine." Compare to what the participants shared regarding their current hygiene routine. |
| | 5. Using the list of hygiene tasks created at the start of this activity, encourage participants to think about their current hygiene routines (if they exist) and any adjustments needed. If needed, support participants through this step with prompts, leading questions, etc. |
| | 6. Write the routines on "My Morning Hygiene Routine" and "My Evening Hygiene Routine." |
| | 7. Make several copies of each participant's completed routines. Laminate, if desired. Post the routines in applicable environments. Encourage participants to use the hygiene routine checklists, practicing with the visual support. Explain that eventually, with enough practice, they will become accustomed to the routine and will be able to fade the visual, depending on their preference.<br><br>**Note: At first, despite the support of the visual, participants may need supervised and assisted practice with their routine.** |

## Needed Materials:

☐ Instructional Materials and Supports:
"My Morning Hygiene Routine" (1 copy per participant)
"My Evening Hygiene Routine" (1 copy per participant)
"Sample Morning Hygiene Routine" (1 copy per participant)
"Sample Evening Hygiene Routine" (1 copy per participant)
☐ Pencils
☐ Large piece of paper or board
☐ Binders
☐ Introduction to Good Hygiene – Lesson Plan 2

# My Morning Hygiene Routine

☐ _____

_____

☐ _____

_____

☐ _____

_____

☐ _____

_____

☐ _____

_____

☐ _____

# My Evening Hygiene Routine

☐ _____

_____

☐ _____

_____

☐ _____

_____

☐ _____

_____

☐ _____

_____

☐ _____

# Sample Morning Hygiene Routine

☐ Brush teeth

☐ Shower:
    ☐ Wet hair and body
    ☐ Shampoo hair and rinse
    ☐ Wash face with soap
    ☐ Wash body with soap

☐ Dry off

☐ Comb hair

☐ Apply deodorant

☐ Put on clean underwear and clothes

☐ Check appearance in mirror:
    ☐ Check hair and re-comb, if needed
    ☐ Check face
    ☐ Check clothing

# Sample Evening Hygiene Routine

☐  Brush teeth

☐  Wash face

☐  Check fingernails and toenails
   ☐   Clip long nails
   ☐   Remove any dirt

☐  Choose clean clothes for next day

☐  Lay clean underwear and outfit for next day in designated place

# Hygiene Activity #5
# "Search and Find and Read Your Mind"

## Instructions:

| | |
|---|---|
| 1. | Using magazines or the Internet and a printer, have each participant find:<br>• Picture of someone with poor hygiene<br>• Picture of someone with good hygiene |
| 2. | Have each participant cut and paste pictures on a "Hygiene Thought Bubble Worksheet" and complete worksheet. |
| 3. | Share the end product with the group. |

## Needed Materials:

☐ Instructional Materials and Supports:

"Hygiene Thought Bubble Worksheet – Homework Version" (2 copies per participant)

☐ Pencils

☐ Scissors

☐ Glue

☐ Binders

☐ Pictures illustrating poor and good hygiene

☐ Printer

☐ Introduction to Good Hygiene – Lesson Plan 2 (homework assignment following Lesson 2)

# Hygiene Thought Bubble Worksheet – Homework Version

## Instructions:

1. Attach a picture in the designated area.
2. Determine if the person in the picture demonstrates socially O.K. hygiene or socially inappropriate hygiene by circling the corresponding answer in the area below.
3. Based on the hygiene of the person in the picture, list the common thoughts and feelings the other person might have in the blank thought bubble provided.

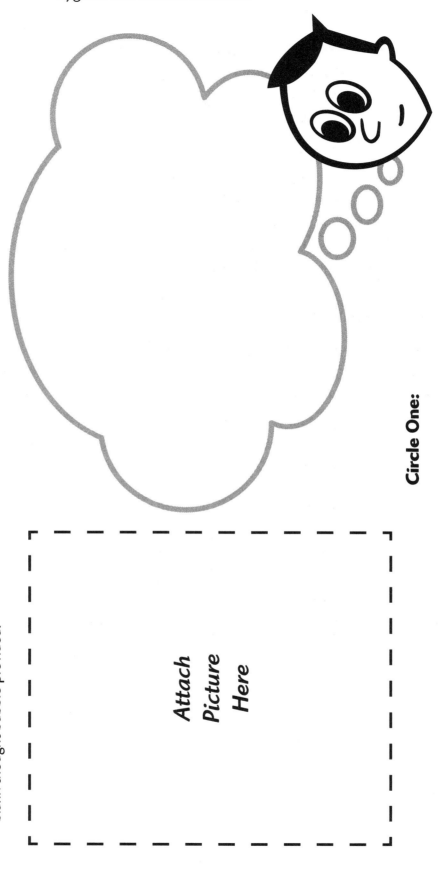

**Circle One:**

**Socially Inappropriate Hygiene**

**Socially O.K. Hygiene**

Attach Picture Here

# Introduction to Good Hygiene – Lesson Plan 3

## Session Schedule to Post:

- Chat and review
- Fun activity – poster
- Game
- Closing (snack, reward, etc.)

## Lesson Details:

| Estimated Time | Activity | Refer to Pages: |
|---|---|---|
| 5 minutes | Opening – Gather participants. Post and review schedule for session | |
| 5 minutes | REVIEW – Have participants share their completed homework assigned during the previous session (Hygiene Activity #5 – "Search and Find and Read Your Mind") | |
| 20 minutes | Hygiene Activity #6 – "Hygiene Poster" | 35 |
| 10 minutes | Hygiene Activity #7 – "Every Vote Counts" | 36-37 |
| 5 minutes | Closing | |

## Needed Materials:

- ☐ Instructional Materials and Supports:
  "Hygiene Voting Cards" (1 "Socially O.K. Hygiene Card" and 1 "Socially Inappropriate Hygiene Card" per participant)
- ☐ 10-15 pictures of people demonstrating good or poor hygiene. Please refer to References and Other Resources for tips on finding pictures
- ☐ "Hygiene Thought Bubble Worksheet" completed during previous session
- ☐ Completed "Hygiene Thought Bubble Worksheet – Homework Version" (to be completed by each participant)
- ☐ *Optional:* Copies of all completed "Hygiene Thought Bubble Worksheets" and "Hygiene Thought Bubble Worksheets – Homework Version" (so participants can keep originals in binders)
- ☐ Pencils
- ☐ Markers
- ☐ Glue
- ☐ Scissors
- ☐ Poster board or large piece of paper
- ☐ Binders

## Following Session, Add to Binder:

Not applicable

# Introduction to Good Hygiene Activity #6
# "Hygiene Poster"

## Instructions:

| | 1. | Gather the completed "Hygiene Thought Bubble Worksheets" from Hygiene Activity #3 – "I Can Read Your Mind" and Activity #5 – "Search and Find and Read Your Mind." |
|---|---|---|
| | 2. | *Optional:* Copy each page so participants can keep originals in their binders. |
| | 3. | Instruct the participants to attach the completed "Hygiene Thought Bubble Worksheets" on a poster board or other large piece of paper. |
| | 4. | Display poster in a central area for quick referral. |

## Needed Materials:

☐ Completed "Hygiene Thought Bubble Worksheets"

☐ *Optional:* Copies of all completed "Hygiene Thought Bubble Worksheets" (so participants can keep originals in binders)

☐ Markers

☐ Glue

☐ Scissors

☐ Poster board or large piece of paper

☐ Pencils

☐ Binders

☐ Introduction to Good Hygiene – Lesson Plan 3

# Introduction to Good Hygiene Activity #7
# "Every Vote Counts"

## Instructions:

| | | |
|---|---|---|
| | 1. | At the start of the game, give each participant 2 Hygiene Voting Cards: 1 "Socially O.K. Hygiene Card" and 1 "Socially Inappropriate Hygiene Card." |
| | 2. | Explain the directions of game. |
| | 3. | Show the first picture of a person with either good hygiene or poor hygiene. |
| | 4. | Have participants vote by raising the card that represents the hygiene habit of the person in the picture. |
| | 5. | The first participant to have the correct answer in the air wins 1 point. |
| | 6. | Repeat Steps 4-5 to continue the game, keeping track of each participant's points. |
| | 7. | At the conclusion of the game, award prizes to the high-point earners. |

## Needed Materials:

☐ Instructional Materials and Supports:

"Hygiene Voting Cards" (1 "Socially O.K. Hygiene Card" and 1 "Socially Inappropriate Hygiene Card" per participant)

☐ 10-15 pictures of people demonstrating a mix of good and poor hygiene habits. Include pictures of people with well-groomed hair, dirty or messy hair, clean nails, long and dirty nails, dirty clothes, clean clothes, dirty face, clean face, gross teeth, etc. Laminate, if desired. Please refer to References and Other Resources for tips on finding pictures

☐ Prizes for winner(s)

☐ Pencils

☐ Binders

☐ Introduction to Good Hygiene – Lesson Plan 3

# Hygiene Voting Cards

## Leader's Instructions:

Cut out each card following the bold line. Glue onto construction paper or other firm paper. Laminate cards. Use for Introduction to Hygiene Activity #7 – "Every Vote Counts."

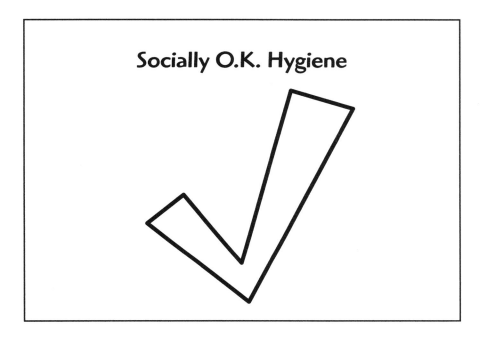

# Introduction to Good Hygiene – Lesson Plan 4

## Session Schedule to Post:

- Chat and review
- Friendly competition
- Wrap-up game
- Closing (snack, reward, etc.)

## Lesson Details:

| Estimated Time | Activity | Refer to Pages: |
|---|---|---|
| 5 minutes | Opening – Gather participants. Post and review schedule for session | |
| 5 minutes | REVIEW – Have participants report their experiences with implementing their hygiene routine during everyday life. Any concerns? Any improvements? Any changes needed? | |
| 20 minutes | Hygiene Activity #8 – "Hygiene Competition" | 39-41 |
| 10 minutes | Hygiene Activity #9 – "Hygiene Wrap-Up" | 42-43 |
| 5 minutes | Closing | |

## Needed Materials:

- ☐ Instructional Materials and Supports:

    "Hygiene Rating Form" (1 copy per participant)

    "Hygiene Rating Form – Sample" (1 copy per participant)

    "Hygiene Wrap-Up – Questions" (1 copy, cut, pasted on firm paper, and laminated)

- ☐ Grand prize for Hygiene Activity #9 – "Hygiene Wrap-Up"
- ☐ Pencils
- ☐ Binders

## Following Session, Add to Binder:

- ☐ "Hygiene Rating Form" – completed version
- ☐ "Hygiene Rating Form – Sample" (1 copy per participant)

# Introduction to Good Hygiene Activity #8
# "Hygiene Competition"

## Instructions:

|   |   |
|---|---|
| | 1. At the start of the game, pass out a copy of "Sample Hygiene Rating Form" to each participant (can use this completed version, or create a rating form personalized for each participant using blank version named "Hygiene Rating Form"). |
| | 2. Explain to participants that they will be partaking in a competition to find the person with the best hygiene habits. |
| | 3. Review the items they will be judged on listed on the "Hygiene Rating Form." |
| | 4. With each participant, complete a "Hygiene Rating Form." Total the checkmarks received and write in the designated area. |
| | 5. Compare all participants' scores to determine winner. |
| | 6. This competition can either be a one-time activity or can be ongoing, monitored on a daily or weekly basis. |

## Needed Materials:

☐ Instructional Materials and Supports:

"Hygiene Rating Form" (1 copy per participant)

"Hygiene Rating Form – Sample" (1 copy per participant)

☐ Pencils

☐ Binders

☐ Introduction to Good Hygiene – Lesson Plan 4

# Sample Hygiene Rating Form

**Leader's Instructions:** Use this rating form for Hygiene Activity #8 – "Hygiene Competition."
*Optional:* Monitor hygiene by completing this checklist each day with the participants. Total the number of ✓'s each participant earns each day and have the participant keep track of her performance. After a designated time period, review all participants' performance and award prizes to highest performers.

| ✓ if completed | Task |
|---|---|
|  | Shower |
|  | Combed hair |
|  | Deodorant |
|  | Teeth brushed |
|  | Short, clean fingernails |
|  | Short, clean toenails |
|  | Clean clothes |
|  | Clean glasses |

**NAME:** _____

**TOTAL ✓'s:** _____

**DATE:** _____

# Hygiene Rating Form

**Leader's Instructions:** Use this rating form for Hygiene Activity #8 – "Hygiene Competition."
*Optional:* Monitor hygiene by completing this checklist each day with the participants. Total the number of ✓'s each participant earns each day and have the participant keep track of her performance. After a designated time period, review all participants' performance and award prizes to highest performers.

| ✓ if completed | Task |
|---|---|
|  |  |
|  |  |
|  |  |
|  |  |
|  |  |
|  |  |
|  |  |
|  |  |

**NAME:** _____

**TOTAL ✓'s:** _____

**DATE:** _____

# Introduction to Good Hygiene Activity #9
# "Hygiene Wrap-Up"

## Instructions:

| | |
|---|---|
| | 1. Prior to the start of the game, spread cards face down on table. |
| | 2. Explain to participants that the objective of the game is to earn at least 6 points. If at least 6 points are earned collectively by the participant or group of participants, they earn a grand prize. |
| | 3. To start game, have a participant choose the first card and read out loud. |
| | 4. Encourage participant to answer the question as thoroughly and accurately as possible. |
| | 5. Award 1 point if answered correctly. |
| | 6. Repeat Steps 4-5 until all cards have been used. |
| | 7. Pass out grand prize if participant or group earned 6 points or more. |

## Needed Materials:

☐ Instructional Materials and Supports:

"Hygiene Wrap-Up Questions" (1 copy, cut, pasted on card stock, and laminated)

☐ Grand prize (1 per participant)

☐ Pencils

☐ Binders

☐ Introduction to Good Hygiene – Lesson Plan 4

# Hygiene Wrap-Up Questions

**Leader's Instructions:** Cut out each question below. Glue onto construction paper or card stock. Laminate cards. Use for Hygiene Activity #9 –"Hygiene Wrap-Up."

1. What does good hygiene mean?

2. Why is good hygiene important?

3. What do you think about someone with good hygiene?

4. What do you think about someone with poor hygiene?

5. What do others think of you when you look and smell clean?

6. What do others think of you when you look and smell dirty?

7. What hygiene activities are important to do daily? Weekly?

<... />

# Chapter 3

# Oral Hygiene

## Chapter Objectives:

- To establish knowledge of good oral hygiene practices.
- To understand the connection between oral hygiene and the thoughts and feelings of others.

# List of Activities

The following is a list of activities included in this chapter. Please refer to the subsequent pages for a complete description of each activity.

1. Introduction to Oral Hygiene – Questions

2. Introduction to Oral Hygiene – Discussion Guide

3. I Can Read Your Mind

4. Fun Oral Hygiene Trivia

5. Egg-Citing Experiment

6. Brushing My Teeth

7. Caught Red-Mouthed

8. Brushing Competition

9. Say Cheese

10. Every Vote Counts

11. Search and Find and Read Your Mind

12. Oral Hygiene Poster

13. My Oral Hygiene Routine

14. Oral Hygiene on the Run

15. Oral Hygiene Wrap-Up

# List of Instructional Materials and Supports

The following is a list of instructional materials and supports that may be used to enhance the activities, and lessons in this chapter. Please refer to the subsequent pages for a copy of each resource.

1. Introduction to Oral Hygiene – Questions

2. Introduction to Oral Hygiene – Discussion Guide

3. Oral Hygiene Thought Bubble Worksheet

4. Fun Oral Hygiene Trivia

5. Fun Oral Hygiene Trivia – Answer Page

6. Sample Teeth-Brushing Rating Form

7. Teeth-Brushing Rating Form

8. Oral Hygiene Voting Cards

9. Oral Hygiene Thought Bubble Worksheet – Homework Version

10. My Oral Hygiene Routine

11. Sample Oral Hygiene Routine

12. Oral Hygiene Scavenger Hunt – List of Objects and Activities

13. Oral Hygiene Wrap-Up Questions

# Oral Hygiene – Lesson Plan 1

### Session Schedule to Post:

- Chat – introduction to oral hygiene
- Fun activity
- Closing (snack, reward, etc.)

### Lesson Details:

| Estimated Time | Activity | Refer to Pages: |
|---|---|---|
| 5 minutes | Opening – Gather participants. Post and review schedule for session | |
| 10 minutes | Oral Hygiene Activity #1 – "Introduction to Oral Hygiene – Questions" | 49-50 |
| 10 minutes | Oral Hygiene Activity #2 – "Introduction to Oral Hygiene – Discussion Guide" to facilitate further discussion and provide any missed information | 51-52 |
| 15 minutes | Oral Hygiene Activity #3 – "I Can Read Your Mind" | 53-54 |
| 5 minutes | Closing | |

### Needed Materials:

- ☐ Instructional Materials and Supports:
  "Introduction to Oral Hygiene – Questions" (1 copy per participant)
  "Introduction to Oral Hygiene – Discussion Guide" (1 copy per participant)
  "Oral Hygiene Thought Bubble Worksheet" (2 copies per participant)
- ☐ Pictures of people demonstrating good and poor oral hygiene. Please refer to References and Other Resources for tips on finding pictures (2 pictures per participant)
- ☐ Pencils
- ☐ Scissors
- ☐ Glue
- ☐ Binders

### Following Session, Add to Binder:

"Introduction to Oral Hygiene – Questions" – completed version
"Introduction to Oral Hygiene – Discussion Guide"
"Oral Hygiene Thought Bubble Worksheet" – completed version

# Oral Hygiene Activity #1
# "Introduction to Oral Hygiene – Questions"

## Instructions:

| | |
|---|---|
| | 1. Give each participant a copy of "Introduction to Oral Hygiene – Questions." |
| | 2. Instruct participants to write answers to the questions on their worksheet. If writing is a source of anxiety or frustration, offer accommodations (i.e., scribe, partner with another participant, etc.). |
| | 3. Set timer for a designated time period, if needed. |
| | 4. When participants are finished, read the first question aloud to the group. |
| | 5. Have participants share their answer. Discuss. |
| | 6. Repeat Steps 4-5 until each question is discussed. |

## Needed Materials:

☐ Instructional Materials and Supports:

"Introduction to Oral Hygiene – Questions" (1 copy per participant)

☐ Pencils

☐ Binders

☐ Oral Hygiene – Lesson Plan 1

# Introduction to Oral Hygiene – Questions

**Instructions:** After reading the questions, write your answers in the space provided.

What does it mean to have good oral hygiene?



How do oral hygiene habits impact the thoughts and feelings of other people?



What tasks should I do to have good oral hygiene?

    1.

    2.

    3.

    4.

    5.



What oral hygiene products should I have available?



What are some potential oral health problems that could arise as a result of poor oral hygiene?

# Oral Hygiene Activity #2
# "Introduction to Oral Hygiene – Discussion Guide"

## Instructions:

| | |
|---|---|
| 1. | Give each participant a copy of "Introduction to Oral Hygiene – Discussion Guide." |
| 2. | Read the first question out loud. |
| 3. | Choose a participant to answer the question by reading the information provided on the worksheet or by expanding on the information on the worksheet. |
| 4. | Challenge the other participants to think of additional information that is not provided on the worksheet. |
| 5. | Repeat Steps 2-4 until all of the questions have been discussed. |

## Needed Materials:

☐ Instructional Materials and Supports:

"Introduction to Oral Hygiene – Discussion Guide" (1 copy per participant)

☐ Pencils

☐ Binders

☐ Oral Hygiene – Lesson Plan 1

# Introduction to Oral Hygiene – Discussion Guide

### What does it mean to have good oral hygiene?

Keeping mouth clean and smelling fresh. Also, taking care of your teeth and gums in order to avoid decay and infections.

### How do oral hygiene habits impact the thoughts and feelings of other people?

If you have good oral hygiene (i.e., clean teeth, fresh breath), others will think more positively about you. If you have poor oral hygiene (i.e., dirty teeth, smelly breath), others will think gross thoughts about you and will most likely not want to interact with you.

### What tasks should I do to have good oral hygiene?

It is important to follow an oral hygiene routine every day that helps you keep your mouth clean. Everyone's oral hygiene routine is a little different, but here are a few important things to think about:

1. **Brush your teeth**
   - Brush your teeth at least 2 times a day – one time in the morning and one time in the afternoon/evening
   - Use toothpaste every time you brush your teeth

2. **Floss**
   - Floss at least one time per day

3. **Monitor your breath**
   - Use mouthwash, gum, and/or mints if breath is offensive
   - Drink plenty of water to keep bad breath at bay

4. **Do frequent checks throughout the day (try to find a mirror)**
   - Check your teeth for food

### What oral hygiene products should I have available?
- Toothbrush
- Toothpaste
- Floss

### What are some potential oral health problems that could arise as a result of poor oral hygiene?
- Develop gum infections
- Develop tooth decay and lose teeth

# Oral Hygiene Activity #3
# "I Can Read Your Mind"

## Instructions:

| | |
|---|---|
| | 1. Give each participant 2 pictures of people demonstrating good and poor oral hygiene. |
| | 2. Have participants cut and glue the first picture on an "Oral Hygiene Thought Bubble Worksheet." |
| | 3. Instruct participants to begin completing the first "Oral Hygiene Thought Bubble Worksheet" by determining if the picture is an example of a socially O.K. oral hygiene or socially inappropriate oral hygiene. |
| | 4. To complete the first "Oral Hygiene Thought Bubble Worksheet," encourage each participant to list the common thoughts and feelings the other person would have, based on the oral hygiene of the person in the picture. Have them write their answers in the blank thought bubble provided. You may need to support participants if they are having difficulty. For example, you can write a list of potential thoughts and feelings on the board and have participants select from the list (to add extra difficulty, provide some correct answers and some answers that are incorrect). |
| | 5. To complete the assignment, instruct participants to repeat Steps 2-4 using the second picture. |
| | 6. When everyone is finished, have each participant share the end product with the group. |

## Needed Materials:

☐ Instructional Materials and Supports:

"Oral Hygiene Thought Bubble Worksheet" (2 copies per participant)

☐ Pictures of people with good and poor oral hygiene. Include pictures of people with clean teeth and some with obvious tooth decay. Please refer to References and Other Resources for tips on finding pictures (2 pictures per participant)

☐ Pencils

☐ Scissors

☐ Glue

☐ Binders

☐ Oral Hygiene – Lesson Plan 1

# Oral Hygiene Thought Bubble Worksheet

## Instructions:

1. Attach a picture in the designated area.
2. Determine if the person in the picture demonstrates socially O.K. oral hygiene or socially inappropriate oral hygiene by circling the corresponding answer in the area below.
3. Based on the oral hygiene of the person in the picture, list the common thoughts and feelings the other person might have in the blank thought bubble provided.

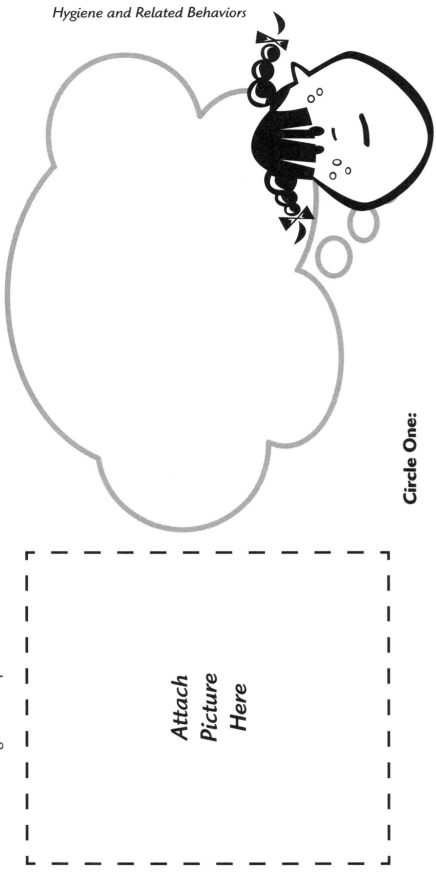

┌ ─ ─ ─ ─ ─ ─ ─ ─ ─ ─ ─ ┐

*Attach*
*Picture*
*Here*

└ ─ ─ ─ ─ ─ ─ ─ ─ ─ ─ ─ ┘

**Socially Inappropriate Oral Hygiene**

**Circle One:**

**Socially O.K. Oral Hygiene**

# Oral Hygiene – Lesson Plan 2

## Session Schedule to Post:

- Chat and review
- Fun trivia
- Experiment
- Closing (snack, reward, etc.)

## Lesson Details:

| Estimated Time | Activity | Refer to Pages: |
|---|---|---|
| 5 minutes | Opening – Gather participants. Post and review schedule for session | |
| 5 minutes | REVIEW – Have participants briefly recall the information covered during the previous session. If needed, refer them to the following forms added to the binders: "Introduction to Oral Hygiene – Questions" and "Introduction to Oral Hygiene – Discussion Guide" | |
| 10 minutes | Oral Hygiene Activity #4 – "Fun Oral Hygiene Trivia" | 56–58 |
| 20 minutes | Oral Hygiene Activity #5 – "Egg-Citing Experiment" | 59 |
| 5 minutes | Closing | |

## Needed Materials:

☐ Instructional Materials and Supports:
"Fun Oral Hygiene Trivia" (1 copy, cut, pasted on index cards and laminated)
"Fun Oral Hygiene Trivia – Answer Page" (1 copy)

☐ 2 Eggshells

☐ 2 Plastic containers – 1 labeled "Socially O.K. Oral Hygiene"; 1 labeled "Socially Inappropriate Oral Hygiene"

☐ Bottle of vinegar labeled "plaque"

☐ Water

☐ Pencils

☐ Markers

☐ Wipe board or large piece of paper

☐ Binders

## Following Session, Add to Binder:

Not applicable

# Oral Hygiene Activity #4
# "Fun Oral Hygiene Trivia"

## Instructions:

|   |   |
|---|---|
| 1. | Spread the index cards face down on table or floor. |
| 2. | Have the first participant pick one card and read the trivia question out loud to the rest of the group. |
| 3. | Encourage the reader to answer the question or make a best guess. |
| 4. | Challenge each of the other participants to guess the answer. |
| 5. | After all participants have had a turn to guess, read the correct answer out loud. |
| 6. | Repeat Steps 3-5 until all of the trivia questions have been discussed. |

## Needed Materials:

☐  1 copy of "Fun Oral Hygiene Trivia" cut, pasted on index cards, and laminated

☐  1 copy of "Fun Oral Hygiene Trivia – Answer Page"

☐  Binders

☐  Oral Hygiene – Lesson Plan 2

# Fun Oral Hygiene Trivia

**Leader's Instructions:** Cut and paste each question on a separate index card. Laminate, if desired. Use for Oral Hygiene Activity #4 – Fun Oral Hygiene Trivia.

Q:    How many permanent teeth do we have?

Q:    What are the 3 main functions of teeth?

Q:    What is the hardest material in the human body?

Q:    What is plaque?

Q:    What is the simplest way to get rid of plaque?

Q:    What was the first form of a toothbrush made of?

Q:    When was the modern toothbrush invented?

Q:    What material was used to make the first type of toothbrush bristle?

Q:    When were the nylon bristles invented (like the bristles used today)?

Q:    When was the first electric toothbrush invented?

# Fun Oral Hygiene Trivia – Answer Page

*Adapted from www.oralb.com and www.crest.com*

**Q:  How many permanent teeth do we have?**

*A:   We typically have 32 permanent teeth.*

**Q:  What are the 3 main functions of teeth?**

*A:   Teeth are designed for:*

- *Chewing, biting and tearing*
- *Speaking clearly*
- *Appearance*

**Q:  What is the hardest material in the human body?**

*A:   Enamel is the outer covering of our teeth. It is the hardest material in the human body.*

**Q:  What is plaque?**

*A:   Plaque is a sticky film of bacteria that constantly forms on our teeth. The bacteria release acid that attacks the enamel and can eventually cause cavities.*

**Q:  What is the simplest way to get rid of plaque?**

*A:   By brushing your teeth.*

**Q:  What was the first form of a toothbrush made of?**

*A:   Ancient civilizations invented the idea of cleaning their teeth by mashing the end of a stick flat and scraping their teeth clean (dated as far back as 3000 B.C.E.).*

**Q:  When was the modern toothbrush invented?**

*A:   The modern toothbrush, with bristles, was conceived in China around 1498.*

**Q:  What material was used to make the first type of toothbrush bristle?**

*A:   Animal hair, particularly hair from the back of a hog's neck, was the first type of bristle to be used.*

**Q:  When were the nylon bristles invented (like the bristles used today)?**

*A:   Animal hair was used until 1938, when nylon bristles were introduced.*

**Q:  When was the first electric toothbrush invented?**

*A:   Electric toothbrushes were invented and marketed in 1880 by "Dr. Scott." The popularity of the electric toothbrush did not take off until after World War II. When the cordless model was invented in 1960, popularity skyrocketed.*

# Oral Hygiene Activity #5
# "Egg-Citing Experiment"

## Instructions:

| | |
|---|---|
| | 1. At the start of the activity, explain to the participants that they are going to perform an experiment that will demonstrate the importance of good oral hygiene. |
| | 2. Have a participant place one empty eggshell in the container marked "Socially O.K. Oral Hygiene" and one empty eggshell in the container marked "Socially Inappropriate Oral Hygiene." |
| | 3. Explain that the eggshells represent our teeth. Point out the labels on the containers. |
| | 4. Have a participant add plaque (vinegar) to the container labeled "Socially Inappropriate Oral Hygiene," completely covering the eggshell. Explain that this represents the natural process of plaque attacking our teeth. |
| | 5. Have a participant add water to the container labeled "Socially O.K. Oral Hygiene." Explain that this represents what happens when we brush and rinse the plaque off our teeth. |
| | 6. Encourage participants to carefully observe the 2 containers. Discuss their observations. The shell soaking in vinegar will start to slowly dissolve, representing the effects of plaque on tooth decay. |
| | 7. Reserve the experiment for several days, keeping it in an area that allows participants to observe the changes throughout the week. |
| | 8. After a few days, discuss the changes that occurred. The container labeled "Socially Inappropriate Oral Hygiene" (with vinegar) should have a completely or closely dissolved eggshell. Emphasize the similarity to plaque attacking teeth. Eventually, if plaque is not properly removed by frequent brushing, teeth will start to decay and dissolve. |

## Needed Materials:

☐ 2 Eggshells

☐ 2 Plastic Containers – 1 labeled "Socially O.K. Oral Hygiene"; 1 labeled "Socially Inappropriate Oral Hygiene"

☐ Bottle of vinegar labeled "plaque"

☐ Water

☐ Pencils

☐ Binders

☐ Oral Hygiene – Lesson Plan 2

# Oral Hygiene – Lesson Plan 3

## Session Schedule to Post:

- Chat and review
- Fun activity – demonstration and experiment
- Friendly competition
- Closing (snack, reward, etc.)

## Lesson Details:

| *Estimated Time* | *Activity* | *Refer to Pages:* |
|---|---|---|
| 5 minutes | Opening – Gather participants. Post and review schedule for session | |
| 1 minute | In preparation for upcoming activity, pass out a sugary snack for participants to enjoy | |
| 5 minutes | REVIEW – Have participants look at the results of the "Egg-citing Experiment" from the previous session (Oral Hygiene Activity #5). Discuss results. Relate results of experiment to oral hygiene concepts | |
| 10 minutes | Oral Hygiene Activity #6 – "Brushing My Teeth" | 61-63 |
| 5 minutes | Oral Hygiene Activity #7 – "Caught Red-Mouthed" | 64 |
| 15 minutes | Oral Hygiene Activity # 8 – "Brushing Competition" | 65 |
| 5 minutes | Closing | |

## Needed Materials:

- ☐ Instructional Materials and Supports:
  "Sample Teeth-Brushing Rating Form" (1 copy per participant)
  "Teeth-Brushing Rating Form" (1 copy per participant)
- ☐ Results of Egg-Citing Experiment (performed during previous lesson)
- ☐ Sugary Snacks
- ☐ Large mouth/teeth model (optional)
- ☐ Red plaque tablets
- ☐ Camera
- ☐ Toothbrushes (1 for each participant + 1 extra for demonstration) and toothpaste
- ☐ Mirror
- ☐ Camera (optional)
- ☐ Pencils
- ☐ Binders

## Following Session, Add to Binder:

- ☐ "Teeth-Brushing Rating Form" – completed version

# Oral Hygiene Activity #6
# "Brushing My Teeth"

## Instructions:

| | |
|---|---|
| | 1. At the start of the activity, give participants a copy of the "Sample Teeth-Brushing Rating Form." Explain that the steps listed on the worksheet are important items to remember each time they brush their teeth. Go over each briefly, and discuss. |
| | 2. Using a toothbrush and model of the mouth/teeth, demonstrate the correct way to brush teeth. Highlight important aspects and, for a visual support, refer participants to the "Sample Teeth-Brushing Rating Form," which covers most of these aspects. |
| | 3. Using a toothbrush and model of the mouth/teeth, encourage each participant to demonstrate the proper way to brush teeth. |
| | 4. As each participant demonstrates on the model, have the remaining participants monitor his or her performance using the criteria on the "Sample Teeth-Brushing Rating Form." |
| | 5. *Optional:* If you wish to use a checklist that is more specific to each participant's needs, complete the blank "Teeth-Brushing Rating Form" and use it during this activity. |

## Needed Materials:

☐ Instructional Materials and Supports:

"Sample Teeth-Brushing Rating Form" (1 copy per participant)

"Teeth-Brushing Rating Form" (1 copy per participant)

☐ Large mouth/teeth model (contact local dentist, school nurse, health teacher to borrow a model for the activity)

☐ Toothbrushes (1 for each participant + 1 extra for demonstration)

☐ Pencils

☐ Binders

☐ Oral Hygiene – Lesson Plan 3

# Sample Teeth-Brushing Rating Form

**Leader's Instructions:** Monitor oral hygiene by completing this checklist. Total the number of ✓'s participants earn and have them keep track of their performance.

| ✓ if completed | Task |
|---|---|
| | Used toothpaste |
| | Brushed front surface of all teeth |
| | Brushed inner surface of all teeth |
| | Brushed top (chewing) surface of all teeth |
| | Brushed tongue |
| | Brushed roof of mouth |
| | Carefully spit toothpaste in sink and rinsed sink |
| | Rinsed mouth well with water |
| | Wiped mouth clean |
| | Rinsed toothbrush and put away paste and brush |

**NAME:** _____

**TOTAL ✓'s:** _____

**DATE:** _____

# Teeth-Brushing Rating Form

**Leader's Instructions:** Monitor oral hygiene by completing this checklist. Total the number of ✓'s participants earn and have them keep track of their performance.

| ✓ if completed | Task |
|---|---|
|  |  |
|  |  |
|  |  |
|  |  |
|  |  |
|  |  |
|  |  |
|  |  |
|  |  |
|  |  |

**NAME:** _____

**TOTAL ✓'s:** _____

**DATE:** _____

# Oral Hygiene Activity #7
# "Caught Red-Mouthed"

## Instructions:

| | | |
|---|---|---|
| | 1. | In the beginning of the activity, encourage each participant to eat a sugary snack (donuts, candy, etc.). |
| | 2. | Several minutes later, give each participant a red tablet to chew (see below). Explain that they are going to do an experiment to find plaque in their mouths. |
| | 3. | After they have chewed the tablet, have participants look in a mirror at the results. Encourage them to look at the other participants' results, too. |
| | 4. | Explain that the tablet shows areas of plaque build-up by highlighting them in red. Encourage each participant to pay close attention to his or her areas of concern. |
| | 5. | *Optional:* Take pictures of their red teeth. |
| | 6. | *Important Note:* This activity is a good precursor to Oral Hygiene Activity #8 – "Brushing Competition." |

## Needed Materials:

☐ Sugary snacks
☐ Red plaque tablets (ask local dentist to donate tablets for purposes of this activity)
☐ Camera
☐ Mirror
☐ Camera (optional)
☐ Pencils
☐ Binders
☐ Oral Hygiene – Lesson Plan 3

# Oral Hygiene Activity #8
# "Brushing Competition"

## Instructions:

| | |
|---|---|
| | 1. *Important Note:* This activity is a good follow-up to Oral Hygiene Activity #7 – "Caught Red-Mouthed." |
| | 2. Distribute a toothbrush and toothpaste to each participant. |
| | 3. Divide participants into groups of 2, or have each participant work independently. |
| | 4. Instruct the first partner or individual to brush his teeth in front of a mirror and sink. |
| | 5. Have the activity leader, the partner, or the individual himself/herself "rate" his/her performance using the "Sample Teeth-Brushing Rating Form." *Note:* If you wish to make tasks more specific to participant's needs, use the blank "Teeth-Brushing Rating Form." |
| | 6. Encourage brushers to be very thorough and, if doing this activity as a follow-up to Oral Hygiene Activity #7 – "Caught Red-Mouthed," remind them to remove red stain by brushing well. |
| | 7. Repeat Steps 4-6 until all participants have brushed their teeth. |
| | 8. Have participants count the number of checks they received on the "Sample Teeth-Brushing Rating Form" and write the number in the space provided. |
| | 9. Award prizes to the participants who scored the highest number of points. |
| | 10. *Optional:* Take pictures of clean teeth. |

## Needed Materials:

☐ Instructional Materials and Supports:

   "Sample Teeth-Brushing Rating Form" (1 copy per participant)

   "Teeth-Brushing Rating Form" (1 copy per participant)

☐ Toothbrushes (1 for each participant)

☐ Toothpaste

☐ Mirror

☐ Sink

☐ Camera (optional)

☐ Pencils

☐ Binders

☐ Oral Hygiene – Lesson Plan 3

# Teeth-Brushing Rating Form

**Leader's Instructions:** Monitor oral hygiene by completing this checklist. Total the number of ✓'s participants earn and have them keep track of their performance.

| ✓ if completed | Task |
|---|---|
|  |  |
|  |  |
|  |  |
|  |  |
|  |  |
|  |  |
|  |  |
|  |  |
|  |  |
|  |  |

**NAME:** _____

**TOTAL ✓'s:** _____

**DATE:** _____

# Sample Teeth-Brushing Rating Form

**Leader's Instructions:** Monitor oral hygiene by completing this checklist. Total the number of ✓'s participants earn and have them keep track of their performance.

| ✓ if completed | Task |
|---|---|
| | Used toothpaste |
| | Brushed front surface of all teeth |
| | Brushed inner surface of all teeth |
| | Brushed top (chewing) surface of all teeth |
| | Brushed tongue |
| | Brushed roof of mouth |
| | Carefully spit toothpaste in sink and rinsed sink |
| | Rinsed mouth well with water |
| | Wiped mouth clean |
| | Rinsed toothbrush and put away paste and brush |

**NAME:** _____

**TOTAL ✓'s:** _____

**DATE:** _____

# Oral Hygiene – Lesson Plan 4

## Session Schedule to Post:

- Chat and review
- Game
- Special assignment
- Closing (snack, reward, etc.)

## Lesson Details:

| Estimated Time | Activity | Refer to Pages: |
|---|---|---|
| 5 minutes | Opening – Gather participants. Post and review schedule for session | |
| 5 minutes | REVIEW – Pass out pictures taken of participants during Oral Hygiene Activity #7 – "Caught Red-Mouthed" and Oral Hygiene Activity # 8 – "Brushing Competition" from previous lesson. Discuss pictures and relate to oral hygiene concepts | |
| 15 minutes | Oral Hygiene Activity #9 – "Say Cheese" | 69 |
| 10 minutes | Oral Hygiene Activity #10 – "Every Vote Counts" | 70-71 |
| 5 minutes | Assign and Explain Oral Hygiene Activity #11 – "Search and Find and Read Your Mind" – DUE next group session | 72-73 |
| 5 minutes | Closing | |

## Needed Materials:

☐ Instructional Materials and Supports:

"Oral Hygiene Voting Cards" (1 "Socially O.K. Oral Hygiene Card" and 1 "Socially Inappropriate Oral Hygiene Card" per participant)

"Oral Hygiene Thought Bubble Worksheet-Homework Version" (2 copies per participant)

☐ Pictures of participants from previous session

☐ 10-15 pictures of people demonstrating good or poor oral hygiene. Please refer to References and Other Resources for tips on finding pictures

☐ Poster board or other large piece of paper

☐ Glue

☐ Scissors

☐ Pencils

☐ Binders

## Following Session, Add to Binder:

Not applicable

# Oral Hygiene Activity #9
# "Say Cheese"

## Instructions:

| | | |
|---|---|---|
| | 1. | Have participants review the pictures taken during Oral Hygiene Activity #7 –"Caught-Red Mouthed" and Oral Hygiene Activity #8 – "Brushing Competition" and compare the differences between each picture. |
| | 2. | Instruct participants to assemble a before and after poster to demonstrate the importance of brushing teeth thoroughly to remove all plaque. |
| | 3. | Display the poster in a central area for quick referral. |

## Needed Materials:

☐ Pictures of participants taken during Oral Hygiene Activity #7 – "Caught-Red Mouthed" and Oral Hygiene Activity #8 – "Brushing Competition." One picture should have been taken directly following the consumption of the red plaque tablet (plaque smile), the other should have been taken directly after participants brushed their teeth (clean smile)

☐ Poster board or other large piece of paper

☐ Glue

☐ Scissors

☐ Markers

☐ Pencils

☐ Tape or other method of securing poster to wall

☐ Binders

☐ Oral Hygiene – Lesson Plan 4

# Oral Hygiene Activity #10 – "Every Vote Counts"

## Instructions:

|  |  |
|---|---|
| | 1. At the start of the game, give each participant 2 Oral Hygiene Voting Cards: 1 "Socially O.K. Hygiene Card" and 1 "Socially Inappropriate Hygiene Card." |
| | 2. Explain the directions of the game. |
| | 3. Show the first picture of a person with either good oral hygiene or poor oral hygiene. |
| | 4. Have participants vote by raising the card that represents the oral hygiene habit of the person in the picture. |
| | 5. The first participant to have the correct answer in the air wins 1 point. |
| | 6. Repeat Steps 4-5 to continue the game, keeping track of each participant's points. |
| | 7. At the conclusion of the game, award prizes to the high-point earners. |

## Needed Materials:

☐ Instructional Materials and Supports:

"Oral Hygiene Voting Cards" (1 "Socially O.K. Oral Hygiene Card" and 1 "Socially Inappropriate Oral Hygiene Card" per participant)

☐ 10-15 pictures of people demonstrating good or poor oral hygiene. Include pictures of people with clean teeth and others with obvious tooth decay. Cut and paste pictures on construction paper or other firm paper. Laminate, if desired. Please refer to References and Other Resources for tips on finding pictures

☐ Pencils

☐ Binders

☐ Oral Hygiene – Lesson Plan 4

# Oral Hygiene Voting Cards

**Leader's Instructions:** Cut out each card following the bold line. Glue onto construction paper or other firm paper. Laminate cards. Use for Oral Hygiene Activity #10 – "Every Vote Counts."

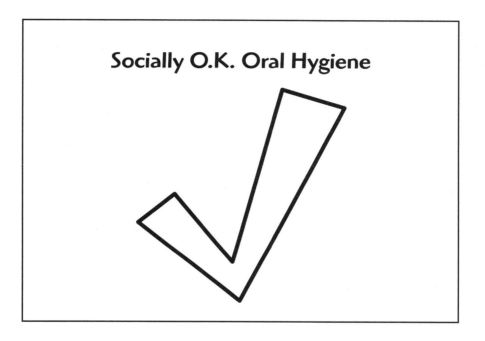

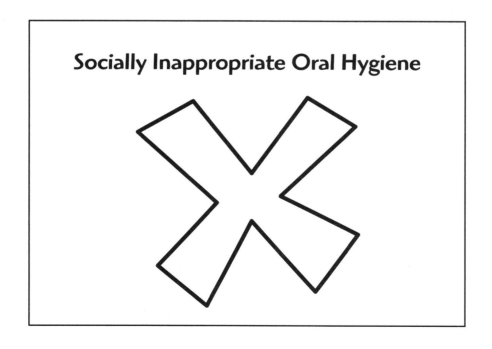

# Oral Hygiene Activity #11
# "Search and Find and Read Your Mind"

## Instructions:

| | |
|---|---|
| | 1. Using magazines or the Internet and a printer, have each participant find:<br>   • Picture of someone with poor oral hygiene<br>   • Picture of someone with good oral hygiene |
| | 2. Have each participant cut and paste each picture on an "Oral Hygiene Thought Bubble Worksheet" and complete the worksheet. |
| | 3. Share the end product with the group. |

## Needed Materials:

☐ Instructional Materials and Supports:

"Oral Hygiene Thought Bubble Worksheet – Homework Version" (2 copies per participant)

☐ Scissors

☐ Glue

☐ Markers

☐ Pencils

☐ Binders

☐ Oral Hygiene – Lesson Plan 4

# Oral Hygiene Thought Bubble Worksheet – Homework Version

## Instructions:

1. Attach a picture in the designated area.
2. Determine if the person in the picture demonstrates socially O.K. oral hygiene or socially inappropriate oral hygiene by circling the corresponding answer in the area below.
3. Based on the oral hygiene of the person in the picture, list the common thoughts and feelings the other person might have in the blank thought bubble provided.

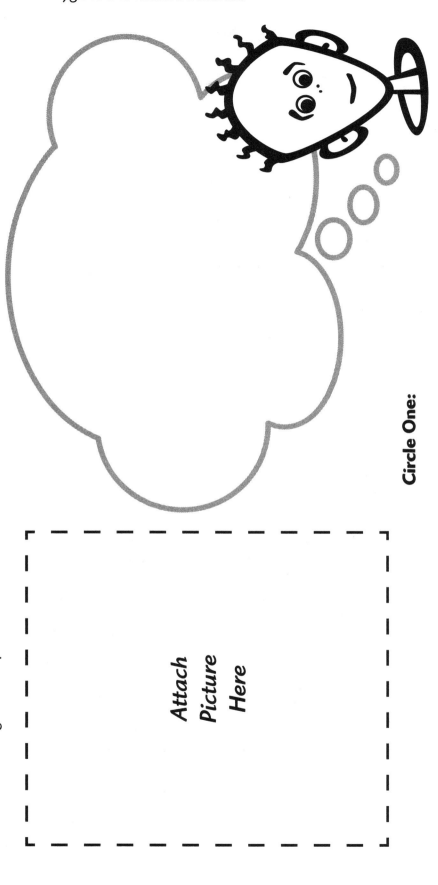

*Attach Picture Here*

**Circle One:**

**Socially Inappropriate Oral Hygiene**

**Socially O.K. Oral Hygiene**

# Oral Hygiene – Lesson Plan 5

## Session Schedule to Post:

- Chat and review
- Fun activity – poster
- Create oral hygiene routine
- Closing (snack, reward, etc.)

## Lesson Details:

| Estimated Time | Activity | Refer to Pages: |
|---|---|---|
| 5 minutes | Opening – Gather participants. Post and review schedule for session | |
| 5 minutes | REVIEW – Have participants share their completed homework that was assigned during the previous session (Oral Hygiene Activity #11 – "Search and Find and Read Your Mind") | |
| 20 minutes | Oral Hygiene Activity #12 – "Oral Hygiene Poster" | 75 |
| 10 minutes | Oral Hygiene Activity #13 – "My Oral Hygiene Routine" | 76-78 |
| 5 minutes | Closing | |

## Needed Materials:

☐ Instructional Materials and Supports:
   "My Oral Hygiene Routine" (1 copy per participant)
   "Sample Oral Hygiene Routine" (1 copy per participant)
☐ "Oral Hygiene Thought Bubble Worksheet" completed during previous activity
☐ Completed "Oral Hygiene Thought Bubble Worksheet – Homework Version" (completed as a homework assignment)
☐ *Optional:* Copies of all completed "Oral Hygiene Thought Bubble Worksheets" and "Oral Hygiene Thought Bubble Worksheets – Homework Version" (so participants can keep originals in binders)
☐ Markers
☐ Glue
☐ Scissors
☐ Poster board or large piece of paper
☐ Pencils
☐ Binders

## Following Session, Add to Binder:

Not applicable

# Oral Hygiene Activity #12
# "Oral Hygiene Poster"

## Instructions:

| | |
|---|---|
| | 1. Gather the completed "Oral Hygiene Thought Bubble Worksheets" from Oral Hygiene Activity #3 – "I Can Read Your Mind" and Oral Hygiene Activity #11 – "Search and Find and Read Your Mind." |
| | 2. *Optional:* Copy each page so participants can keep originals in their binders. |
| | 3. Instruct the participants to attach the completed "Oral Hygiene Thought Bubble Worksheets" to a poster board or large piece of paper. |
| | 4. Display poster in a central area for quick referral. |

## Needed Materials:

☐ Completed "Oral Hygiene Thought Bubble Worksheets"

☐ *Optional:* copies of all completed "Oral Hygiene Thought Bubble Worksheets" (so participants can keep originals in binders)

☐ Markers

☐ Glue

☐ Scissors

☐ Poster board or large piece of paper

☐ Pencils

☐ Binders

☐ Oral Hygiene – Lesson Plan 5

# Oral Hygiene Activity #13
# "My Oral Hygiene Routine"

## Instructions:

| | |
|---|---|
| | 1. Using input from participants, generate a list on the board or a large piece paper of all the tasks that are important for maintaining good hygiene. If needed, refer participants to "Introduction to Good Hygiene – Discussion Guide" (used during Oral Hygiene Activity #2). |
| | 2. Give each participant a copy of:<br>• "My Oral Hygiene Routine"<br>• "Sample Oral Hygiene Routine" |
| | 3. Lead a discussion about oral hygiene routines, explaining that most people develop a consistent routine or hygiene schedule that allows them to complete necessary tasks in a time-efficient and organized manner. Also, following a consistent routine can ensure that important tasks needed for good oral hygiene are not missed. Discuss the importance of this routine and ask participants to briefly share their routines with the group. |
| | 4. Review the sample routine outlined on "Sample Oral Hygiene Routine." Compare to what the participants shared regarding their current oral hygiene routines. |
| | 5. Using the list of oral hygiene tasks created at the start of this activity, encourage participants to think about their current oral hygiene routines (if they exist) and consider any adjustments needed. Support participants through this step with prompts or leading questions. |
| | 6. Write the routines on "My Oral Hygiene Routine." |
| | 7. Make several copies of each participant's completed routines. Laminate, if desired. Post the routines in applicable environments. Encourage participants to use the oral hygiene routine checklists, practicing with the visual support. Explain that eventually, with enough practice, they will become accustomed to the routine and will be able to fade the visual, depending on their preference.<br><br>**Note: At first, despite the support of the visual, participants may need supervised and assisted practice of their routine.** |

## Needed Materials:

☐ Instructional Materials and Supports:

"My Oral Hygiene Routine" (1 copy per participant)

"Sample Oral Hygiene Routine" (1 copy per participant)

☐ Pencils

☐ Binders

☐ Oral Hygiene – Lesson Plan 5

# My Oral Hygiene Routine

☐ _____

_____

☐ _____

_____

☐ _____

_____

☐ _____

_____

☐ _____

_____

☐ _____

_____

# Sample Oral Hygiene Routine

☐    Wet toothbrush

☐    Put a stripe of toothpaste on toothbrush

☐    Brush teeth:
       ☐   Brush teeth on top
       ☐   Brush teeth on bottom
       ☐   Brush tongue

☐    Spit toothpaste in sink

☐    Rinse mouth with water

☐    Rinse sink (making sure all toothpaste is washed away)

☐    Wipe face with towel

☐    Check appearance in mirror (make sure your face is clean)

*Optional: May need to add flossing, rinsing with mouthwash, etc.*

# Oral Hygiene – Lesson Plan 6

## Session Schedule to Post:

- Chat and review
- Fun activity – scavenger hunt
- Wrap-up game
- Closing (snack, reward, etc.)

## Lesson Details:

| Estimated Time | Activity | Refer to Pages: |
|---|---|---|
| 5 minutes | Opening – Gather participants. Post and review schedule for session | |
| 5 minutes | REVIEW – Have participants report their experiences with implementing their oral hygiene routine during everyday life. Any concerns? Any improvements? Any changes needed? | |
| 20 minutes | Oral Hygiene Activity #14 – "Oral Hygiene on the Run" | 80-81 |
| 10 minutes | Oral Hygiene Activity #15 – "Oral Hygiene Wrap-Up" | 82-83 |
| 5 minutes | Closing | |

## Needed Materials:

☐ Instructional Materials and Supports:

"Oral Hygiene Scavenger Hunt – List of Objects and Activities" (1 copy per participant)

"Oral Hygiene Wrap-Up Questions" (1 copy – cut, pasted on firm paper, and laminated)

☐ Items for scavenger hunt: mirror, water, mints, gum, breath spray, mouthwash, toothpaste, toothbrush, paper bag (1 of each item per participant)

☐ Grand prizes for Oral Hygiene Activity #15 – "Oral Hygiene Wrap-Up"

☐ Pencils

☐ Binders

## Following Session, Add to Binder:

☐ "Oral Hygiene Scavenger Hunt – List of Objects and Activities" – completed version

# Oral Hygiene Activity #14
# "Oral Hygiene on the Run"

## Instructions:

| | | |
|---|---|---|
| | 1. | Prior to the start of the game, hide the objects included in the scavenger hunt. |
| | 2. | At the start of the activity, divide participants into groups of 2 (activity can also be completed individually). |
| | 3. | Explain the activity and set parameters based on the unique qualities of the environment (e.g., stay in the classroom, stay in house, do not open the objects found until coming back to the table). |
| | 4. | Go over activities and objects listed on "Scavenger Hunt – List of Objects and Activities" and discuss the importance of each item when striving for good oral hygiene. |
| | 5. | Start the scavenger hunt and closely monitor participants' progress. |
| | 6. | After all participants have completed the activity, gather as a group and determine the winner based on time, objects found, activities completed, etc. |

## Needed Materials:

☐ Instructional Materials and Supports:

"Oral Hygiene Scavenger Hunt – List of Objects and Activities" (1 copy per participant)

☐ Items for scavenger hunt: mirror, water, mints, gum, breath spray, mouthwash, toothpaste, toothbrush, paper bag (1 of each item per participant)

☐ Pencils

☐ Binders

☐ Oral Hygiene – Lesson Plan 6

# Oral Hygiene Scavenger Hunt –
# List of Objects and Activities

**Instructions:** Place a checkmark next to each object or activity once it is completed.

| ✓ When completed | Object or Activity |
|---|---|
| | 1. Check teeth in the mirror |
| | 2. Freshen breath with water |
| | 3. Find a mint |
| | 4. Find a pack of gum |
| | 5. Find breath spray |
| | 6. Find bottle of mouthwash |
| | 7. Find toothpaste |
| | 8. Find toothbrush |

# Oral Hygiene Activity #15
# "Oral Hygiene Wrap-Up"

## Instructions:

| | | |
|---|---|---|
| | 1. | Before the start of the game, spread cards face down on table. |
| | 2. | Explain to participants that the objective of the game is for them to earn at least 6 points. If at least 6 points are earned collectively by a participant or group of participants, they will earn a grand prize. |
| | 3. | To start the game, have a participant choose the first card and read it out loud. |
| | 4. | Encourage participants to answer the question as thoroughly and accurately as possible. |
| | 5. | Award 1 point if answered correctly. |
| | 6. | Repeat Steps 4-5 until all cards have been used. |
| | 7. | Pass out grand prize if 6 points were earned by a participant or the group of participants. |

## Needed Materials:

☐ Instructional Materials and Supports:

"Oral Hygiene Wrap-Up Questions" (1 copy – cut, pasted on firm paper, and laminated)

☐ Grand prizes

☐ Pencils

☐ Binders

☐ Oral Hygiene – Lesson Plan 6

# Oral Hygiene Wrap-Up Questions

**Leader's Instructions:** Cut out each question and glue onto construction paper or other firm paper. Laminate cards. Use for Oral Hygiene Activity #15 – "Oral Hygiene Wrap-Up."

1. What does oral hygiene mean?

2. Why is oral hygiene important?

3. What do you think about someone with clean teeth?

4. What do you think about someone with good breath?

5. What do you think about someone with dirty teeth?

6. What do you think about someone with bad breath?

7. What do others think of you when you have good oral hygiene?

8. What do others think of you when you have poor oral hygiene?

9. What oral hygiene activities are important to do daily?

# Chapter 4

# Picking

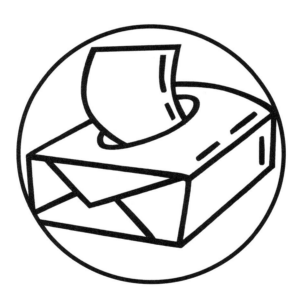

# List of Activities

The following is a list of activities included in this chapter. Please refer to the subsequent pages for a complete description of each activity.

1. Introduction to Picking – Questions

2. Introduction to Picking – Discussion Guide

3. I Can Read Your Mind

4. Fun Picking Trivia

5. Movie Clips

6. Picking Poster

7. People and Places – The Ins and Outs of Picking

8. Pin the Tissue on the Nose

9. Finger vs. Tissue

10. Reaction Time

11. Picking Wrap-Up

# List of Instructional Materials and Supports

The following is a list of instructional materials and supports that may be used to enhance the activities, games, and lessons in this chapter. Please refer to the subsequent pages for a copy of each resource.

1. Introduction to Picking – Questions

2. Introduction to Picking – Discussion Guide

3. Picking Thought Bubble Worksheet

4. Fun Picking Trivia

5. Fun Picking Trivia – Answer Page

6. The Ins and Outs of Picking – Places

7. The Ins and Outs of Picking – People

8. Pin the Tissue on the Nose Poster

9. Finger vs. Tissue Voting Cards

10. Picking Voting Cards

11. Reaction Time Game Cards – Dealing with Picking

12. Picking Wrap-Up Questions

# Picking – Lesson Plan 1

## Session Schedule to Post:

- Chat – introduction to picking
- Fun activity
- Closing (snack, reward, etc.)

## Lesson Details:

| Estimated Time | Activity | Refer to Pages: |
|---|---|---|
| 5 minutes | Opening – Gather participants. Post and review schedule for session | |
| 10 minutes | Picking Activity #1 – "Introduction to Picking – Questions" | 89–90 |
| 10 minutes | Picking Activity #2 – "Introduction to Picking – Discussion Guide" to facilitate further discussion and provide any missed information | 91–92 |
| 15 minutes | Picking Activity #3 – "I Can Read Your Mind" | 93–94 |
| 5 minutes | Closing | |

## Needed Materials:

☐ Instructional Materials and Supports:

"Introduction to Picking – Questions" (1 copy per participant)

"Introduction to Picking – Discussion Guide" (1 copy per participant)

"Picking Thought Bubble Worksheet" (2 copies per participant)

☐ Pictures of people demonstrating a mix of good and poor picking habits. Cut and paste pictures on construction paper or other firm paper. Laminate, if desired. Please refer to References and Other Resources for tips on finding pictures (2 pictures per participant)

☐ Pencils

☐ Binders

## Following Session, Add to Binder:

☐ "Introduction to Picking – Questions" – completed version

☐ "Introduction to Picking – Discussion Guide"

☐ "Picking Thought Bubble Worksheets" – completed version

# Picking Activity #1
# "Introduction to Picking – Questions"

## Instructions:

|   | |
|---|---|
| | 1. Give each participant a copy of "Introduction to Picking – Questions." |
| | 2. Instruct participants to write answers to the questions on their worksheet. If writing is a source of anxiety or frustration, offer accommodations (scribe, partner with another participant, etc.). |
| | 3. Set timer for a designated time period, if needed. |
| | 4. When participants are finished, read the first question aloud to the group. |
| | 5. Have participants share their answer. Discuss. |
| | 6. Repeat Steps 4–5 until each question has been discussed. |

## Needed Materials:

☐ Instructional Materials and Supports:

"Introduction to Picking – Questions" (1 copy per participant)

☐ Pencils

☐ Binders

☐ Picking – Lesson Plan 1

# Introduction to Picking – Questions

**Instructions:** After reading the question, write your answer in the space provided.

What areas on the body do people normally "pick"?

What does it mean to have socially O.K. picking habits?

How do your picking behaviors impact the thoughts and feelings of other people?

What social rules regarding picking are important to follow if you want to make a good impression?

    1.

    2.

    3.

    4.

    5.

    6.

# Picking Activity #2
# "Introduction to Picking – Discussion Guide"

## Instructions:

| | | |
|---|---|---|
| | 1. | Give each participant a copy of "Introduction to Picking – Discussion Guide." |
| | 2. | Read the first question out loud. |
| | 3. | Choose a participant to answer the question by reading the information provided on the worksheet or by expanding on the information on the worksheet. |
| | 4. | Challenge the other participants to think of additional information that is not provided on the worksheet. |
| | 5. | Repeat Steps 2–4 until all of the questions have been discussed. |

## Needed Materials:

☐ Instructional Materials and Supports

    "Introduction to Picking – Discussion Guide" (1 copy per participant)

☐ Pencils

☐ Binders

☐ Picking – Lesson Plan 1

# Introduction to Picking – Discussion Guide

### What areas on the body do people normally "pick"?

Nose, teeth, scabs, acne, fingernails, hangnails, ear, butt ("wedgie"), etc.

### What does it mean to have socially O.K. picking habits?

Assessing where you are and whom you are with to determine if it is socially O.K. to pick a certain body part (e.g., nose).

### How do your picking behaviors impact the thoughts and feelings of other people?

If you have socially O.K. picking habits, others will think more positively about you. If you have inappropriate picking habits, others will think gross thoughts about you and will most likely not want to interact with you.

### What social rules regarding picking are important to follow if you want to make a good impression?

1. It is only O.K. to pick around others if you are in the company of people that you know really well.

2. If you feel something in your nose and other people are around, use a tissue, or go to a private area.

3. If you feel something in your teeth and other people are around, use a toothpick or dental floss, or go to a private area.

4. If you see someone else picking his or her nose, teeth, pimples, etc., ignore it.

5. If you have pimples, scabs, etc., try your best not to pick them. If you absolutely need to pick them, do so in private.

### What are the health risks of picking?

If you pick a pimple, hangnail, or scab, bacteria can enter the open area and an infection could develop. Putting your finger in your nose or mouth can transfer germs from your finger to your nose/mouth, thus making you susceptible to illness.

# Picking Activity #3
# "I Can Read Your Mind"

## Instructions:

| | | |
|---|---|---|
| ☐ | 1. | Give participant 2 pictures of people demonstrating good and poor picking habits. |
| ☐ | 2. | Have participants cut and glue the first picture on a "Picking Thought Bubble Worksheet." |
| ☐ | 3. | Instruct participants to begin completing the first "Picking Thought Bubble Worksheet" by determining if the picture is an example of socially O.K. picking or socially inappropriate picking. |
| ☐ | 4. | To complete the first "Picking Thought Bubble Worksheet," encourage participants to list the common thoughts and feelings the other person would have, based on the picking behavior of the person in the picture. Have them write their answers in the blank thought bubble. You may need to support participants if they are having difficulty. For example, you can write a list of potential thoughts and feelings on the board and have participants select from the list (to add difficulty, provide some correct answers and some answers that are incorrect). |
| ☐ | 5. | To complete the assignment, instruct participants to repeat Steps 2-4 using the second picture. |
| ☐ | 6. | When everyone is finished, have each participant share the end product with the group. |

## Needed Materials:

☐ Instructional Materials and Supports:

"Picking Thought Bubble Worksheet" (2 copies per participant)

☐ Pictures of people demonstrating a mix of good and poor picking habits; include pictures of people using a tissue, picking their nose, picking their teeth, using dental floss, etc. Please refer to References and Other Resources for tips on finding pictures (2 pictures per participant)

☐ Pencils

☐ Scissors

☐ Glue

☐ Binders

☐ Picking – Lesson Plan 1

# Picking Thought Bubble Worksheet

## Instructions:

1. Attach a picture in the designated area.
2. Determine if the person in the picture demonstrates socially O.K. picking or socially inappropriate picking by circling the corresponding answer in the area below.
3. Based on the picking behavior of the person in the picture, list the common thoughts and feelings the other person might have in the blank thought bubble provided.

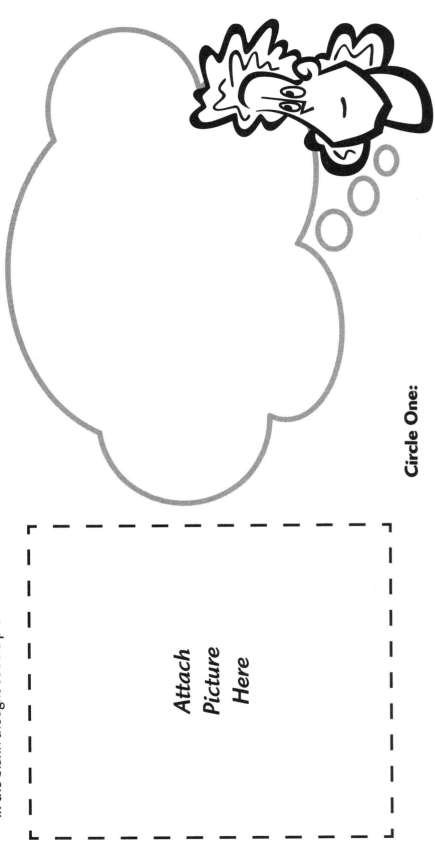

Attach
Picture
Here

**Circle One:**

Socially Inappropriate Picking

Socially O.K. Picking

# Picking – Lesson Plan 2

## Session Schedule to Post:

- Chat and review
- Fun trivia
- Movie clips
- Closing (snack, reward, etc.)

## Lesson Details:

| Estimated Time | Activity | Refer to Pages: |
|---|---|---|
| 5 minutes | Opening – Gather participants. Post and review schedule for session | |
| 5 minutes | REVIEW – Have participants briefly recall the information covered during the previous session. If needed, refer them to the following forms added to the binders: "Introduction to Picking – Questions" and "Introduction to Picking – Discussion Guide" | |
| 10 minutes | Picking Activity #4 – "Fun Picking Trivia" | 96-99 |
| 20 minutes | Picking Activity #5 – "Movie Clips" | 100 |
| 5 minutes | Closing | |

## Needed Materials:

☐ Instructional Materials and Supports:
"Fun Picking Trivia" (1 copy, cut, pasted on index cards, and laminated)
"Fun Picking Trivia – Answer Page" (1 copy)
☐ Movie clips of people demonstrating picking behaviors. Please refer to References and Other Resources for tips regarding movie clips
☐ Computer or other means of playing video clips
☐ Pencils
☐ Markers
☐ Scissors
☐ Glue
☐ Binders

## Following Session, Add to Binder:

☐ "Picking Thought Bubble Worksheet" – completed version

# **Picking Activity #4**
# **"Fun Picking Trivia"**

## **Instructions:**

| | | |
|---|---|---|
| | 1. | At the start of activity, spread the index cards face down on table or floor. |
| | 2. | Have the first participant pick one card and read the trivia question out loud to the rest of the group. |
| | 3. | Encourage the reader to answer the question or share her best guess. |
| | 4. | Challenge each of the other participants to guess the answer. |
| | 5. | After each participant has had a turn to guess, read the correct answer out loud. |
| | 6. | Repeat Steps 3-5 until all of the trivia questions have been discussed. |

## **Needed Materials:**

☐ 1 copy of "Fun Picking Trivia," cut, pasted on index cards, and laminated

☐ 1 copy of "Fun Picking Trivia – Answer Page"

☐ Binders

☐ Picking – Lesson Plan 2

# Fun Picking Trivia

**Leader's Instructions:** Cut and paste each question on a separate index card. Laminate, if desired. Use for Picking Activity #4 – "Fun Picking Trivia."

Q: What are boogers made of?

Q: Does everyone get boogers?

Q: How much snot does your nose make every day?

Q: What did people use to blow their nose in before the invention of Kleenex?

Q: When was the first Kleenex made and what material was it made of?

Q: What makes you sneeze?

Q: When you sneeze, how fast do the particles leave your nose?

Q: When was the toothpick invented?

Q: When was dental floss invented?

Q: What causes acne?

Q: How many people experience acne?

Q: What is a hangnail?

# Fun Picking Trivia – Answer Page

*Adapted from www.oralb.com and www.crest.com*

**Q: What are boogers made of?**

A: *Boogers are made of mucus. Mucus is the thin, slippery material that is found inside your nose. Many people call mucus "snot." When you inhale air through your nose, it contains lots of tiny particles, like dust, dirt, germs, and pollen. If these particles made it all the way to your lungs, the lungs could get damaged, and it would be difficult to breathe. Snot works by trapping the particles and keeping them in the nose. After these particles get stuck inside the nose, the mucus surrounds them along with some of the tiny hairs inside the nose called cilia. The mucus dries around the particles. When the particles and dried-out mucus clump together, you're left with a booger!*

**Q: Does everyone get boogers?**

A: *Yes. Everyone gets boogers.*

**Q: How much snot does your nose make every day?**

A: *Nearly a cupful.*

**Q: What did people use to blow their nose with before the invention of Kleenex?**

A: *Handkerchiefs made of cloth.*

**Q: When was the first Kleenex made and what material was it made of?**

A: *The Kleenex was created in 1924 and was originally marketed as a way to remove cold cream. After many customers suggested that the facial tissues could be used for hay fevers and colds, Kimberly-Clark marketed the slogan "Don't Carry a Cold in Your Pocket" to promote the disposable handkerchief.*

**Q: What makes you sneeze?**

A: *A sneeze is caused by something irritating or tickling the inside of your nose. Most anything that can irritate the inside of your nose can start a sneeze. Some common things include dust, cold air, or pepper. Sneezing is your body's way of removing an irritation from your nose.*

**Q: When you sneeze, how fast do the particles leave your nose?**

A: *Sneezing can send tiny particles speeding out of your nose at up to 100 miles per hour!*

**Q: When was the toothpick invented?**

A: *At least 1.7 million years ago. A molar found from a prehistoric human shows unmistakable evidence of repeated probing by a sharp piece of wood or bone*

**Q: When was dental floss invented?**

A: *Levi Spear Parmly, a New Orleans dentist, is credited as being the inventor of modern dental floss. Parmly promoted teeth flossing with a piece of silk thread in 1815.*

**Q: What causes acne?**

A: *Acne usually appears on your face, back, shoulders, and chest. Pimples form when your pores get clogged (your skin has thousands of individual pores; each pore consists of a hair follicle and a sebaceous – or oil-producing – gland). Clogging can be a result of: dead skin cells building up, bacteria accumulation, overproduction of oil by the sebaceous gland (the result of hormonal changes), and/or oily, pore-clogging products (make up, moisturizers, etc.).*

*Clogging occurs when the sebum, or oil, produced by the sebaceous gland cannot leave the pore as it normally would (to moisturize the skin and hair). An obstruction forms in the pore. The skin around the pore may swell and a white plug (made of dead cells and oil) may form – this is a whitehead. If the plug doesn't fully close the pore, you can get a blackhead.*

**Q: How many people experience acne?**

A: *Acne is most common during adolescence, affecting more than 85% of teenagers, and frequently continues into adulthood.*

**Q: What is a hangnail?**

A: *A hangnail is a small piece of skin at the side or the base of a fingernail that is partly detached from the rest of the skin. Pulling it off can result in an infection.*

# Picking Activity #5
# "Movie Clips"

## Instructions:

| | |
|---|---|
| 1. | Start the activity by showing the first movie clip. Carefully note each participant's reaction, to be used during upcoming discussion. |
| 2. | Have each participant share his or her impression of the person in the video clip. Use the following questions to guide the discussion:<br>• What was your initial reaction to the person's behavior (use observations from Step 1 for reinforcement)?<br>• What were you thinking about that person and his behavior?<br>• What were other people in the clip thinking about the person who was picking? |
| 3. | Continue Steps 1–2 until participants have viewed all clips. |
| 4. | After watching all of the clips, discuss the prevalence of picking clips on the Internet or in movies. Discuss how these clips are often included to interject some humor and that many people find them funny. It is important to stress that it becomes much different when such picking behaviors occur during a real-life situation. Encourage participants to determine the difference between picking behaviors in a movie and in real life. To guide this discussion, use the following questions:<br>• Why are these clips so prevalent?<br>• Do a lot of people find the clips funny?<br>• What is the difference between the people in the clips and in real-life situations?<br>• When is it funny to pick in real life?<br>• When is it NOT funny to pick in real life? |

## Needed Materials:

☐ Movie clips of people demonstrating picking behaviors. Please refer to References and Other Resources for tips regarding movie clips

☐ Computer or other means of playing video clips

☐ Binders

☐ Picking – Lesson Plan 2

# Picking – Lesson Plan 3

## Session Schedule to Post:

- Chat and review
- Fun activity – poster
- Brainstorming session
- Closing (snack, reward, etc.)

## Lesson Details:

| Estimated Time | Activity | Refer to Pages: |
|---|---|---|
| 5 minutes | Opening – Gather participants. Post and review schedule for session | |
| 5 minutes | REVIEW – Have group review the "Picking Thought Bubble Worksheets" from previous session | |
| 10 minutes | Picking Activity #6 – "Picking Poster" | 102 |
| 20 minutes | Picking Activity #7 – "People and Places – The Ins and Outs of Picking" | 103-105 |
| 5 minutes | Closing | |

## Needed Materials:

☐ Instructional Materials and Supports:
"The Ins and Outs of Picking – Places" (1 copy per participant)
"The Ins and Outs of Picking – People" (1 copy per participant)

☐ "Picking Thought Bubble Worksheets" completed during previous lesson plan
*Optional:* Copies of all completed "Picking Thought Bubble Worksheets" (so participants can keep originals in binders)

☐ Pencils

☐ Scissors

☐ Glue

☐ Markers

☐ Poster board or other large piece of paper (for Picking Activity #6 – "Picking Poster")

☐ 2 large pieces of paper, each divided in half by drawing a line down the center (for Picking Activity #7 – "People and Places – The Ins and Outs of Picking"). On the first piece of paper – label one side "Socially O.K. Places" and the other side "Socially Inappropriate Places." On the second piece of paper, label one side "Socially O.K. People" and the other side, "Socially Inappropriate People"

☐ Binders

## Following Session, Add to Binder:

☐ "People and Places – The Ins and Outs of Picking" – completed version

# Picking Activity #6
## "Picking Poster"

## Instructions:

|   |   |
|---|---|
|   | 1. Gather the completed "Picking Thought Bubble Worksheets" from Picking Activity #3 – "I Can Read Your Mind." |
|   | 2. *Optional:* Copy each page so participants can keep originals in their binders. |
|   | 3. Instruct the participants to attach the completed "Picking Thought Bubble Worksheets" on a poster board or other large piece of paper. |
|   | 4. Display poster in a central area for quick referral. |

## Needed Materials:

☐ Completed "Picking Thought Bubble Worksheets"

*Optional:* Copies of all completed "Picking Thought Bubble Worksheets" (so participants can keep originals in binders)

☐ Markers

☐ Glue

☐ Scissors

☐ Poster board or large piece of paper

☐ Pencils

☐ Binders

☐ Picking – Lesson Plan 3

# Picking Activity #7
# "People and Places – The Ins and Outs of Picking"

## Instructions:

| | | |
|---|---|---|
| | 1. | Before the start of the activity, position the participants so that everyone can see the large sheet of paper (hang on wall for easiest viewing). |
| | 2. | Give each participant a copy of "People and Places – The Ins and Outs of Picking." Instruct them to follow along with the activity and write the answers in the appropriate sections. |
| | 3. | Introduce the activity using the following discussion questions:<br>• Are there situations where nose-picking, teeth-picking, etc., are considered socially O.K.? How do you determine if it is socially O.K.?<br>• Are there situations where nose-picking, teeth-picking, etc., are considered socially inappropriate? How do you determine if it is socially inappropriate? |
| | 4. | Start the brainstorming session by asking participants to list places where it is considered socially O.K. to pick. Write the answers in the designated section on the paper. |
| | 5. | Remind participants to write answers on their worksheets. |
| | 6. | Ask participants to brainstorm places where it is socially inappropriate to pick. Write the answers in the designated section on the paper. |
| | 7. | Remind participants to write answers on their worksheets. |
| | 8. | Repeat Steps 4-7, brainstorming people that are socially O.K. and socially inappropriate to pick around. |

## Needed Materials:

☐ Instructional Materials and Supports:

"The Ins and Outs of Picking – Places" (1 copy per participant)

"Then Ins and Outs of Picking – People" (1 copy per participant)

☐ Markers

☐ 2 large pieces of paper, each divided in half by drawing a line down the center. On the first piece of paper, label one side "Socially O.K. Places" and the other, "Socially Inappropriate Places." On the second piece of paper, label one side "Socially O.K. People" and the other, "Socially Inappropriate People"

☐ Tape to hang paper

☐ Pencils

☐ Binders

☐ Picking – Lesson Plan 3

# The Ins and Outs of Picking – Places

**Instructions:** Write answers generated from Picking Activity #7 – "People and Places – The Ins and Outs of Picking" in the spaces provided below.

| Socially O.K. Places | Socially Inappropriate Places |
|---|---|
| 1. | 1. |
| 2. | 2. |
| 3. | 3. |
| 4. | 4. |
| 5. | 5. |
| 6. | 6. |
| 7. | 7. |
| 8. | 8. |

# The Ins and Outs of Picking – People

**Instructions:** Write answers generated from Picking Activity #7 – "People and Places – The Ins and Outs of Picking" in the spaces provided below.

| Socially O.K. People | Socially Inappropriate People |
|---|---|
| 1. | 1. |
| 2. | 2. |
| 3. | 3. |
| 4. | 4. |
| 5. | 5. |
| 6. | 6. |
| 7. | 7. |
| 8. | 8. |

# Picking – Lesson Plan 4

## Session Schedule to Post:

- Chat and review
- Active game
- Game at table
- Closing (snack, reward, etc.)

## Lesson Details:

| Estimated Time | Activity | Refer to Pages: |
|---|---|---|
| 5 minutes | 1. Opening – Gather participants. Post and review schedule for session | |
| 5 minutes | 2. REVIEW – Review posters on display created during Picking Activity #7 – "People and Places – The Ins and Outs of Picking" from previous lesson | |
| 20 minutes | 3. Picking Activity #8 – "Pin the Tissue on the Nose" | 107-108 |
| 10 minutes | 4. Picking Activity #9 – "Finger vs. Tissue" | 109-110 |
| 5 minutes | 5. Closing | |

## Needed Materials:

☐ Instructional Materials and Supports:
"Picking Voting Cards" (1 "Finger Is O.K. Card" and 1 "Use Tissue Card" per participant)
"Pin the Tissue on the Nose Poster" (1 Copy)

☐ Easy view of posters created during Picking Activity #7 – "People and Places – The Ins and Outs of Picking" from previous lesson

☐ Tissues (1 per participant)

☐ Tape

☐ Blindfold

☐ 10-15 pictures of various environments frequented by participants, glued on firm paper and labeled "Specifying Environment Pictured." These can be actual pictures taken in each environment or pictures found on the Internet or in magazines that represent each of these places. Cut and paste pictures of each environment on construction paper or other firm paper. Label each card to specify environment. Laminate cards, if desired

☐ Prize for winner(s) of Picking Activity #9 – "Finger vs. Tissue"

☐ Pencils

☐ Binders

## Following Session, Add to Binder:

Not applicable

# Picking Activity #8 – "Pin the Tissue on the Nose"

## Instructions:

|   |   |
|---|---|
| | 1. Before the start of the game, instruct participants to stand in a single-file line starting approximately 10 feet from the poster hanging on the wall. |
| | 2. Give each participant a tissue with a piece of tape on the end. |
| | 3. Blindfold the first participant (please be aware and sensitive to the unique sensory difficulties of each participant). |
| | 4. Spin the participant in 2-3 circles and point her in the general direction of the poster. |
| | 5. Encourage the participant to walk towards the poster and attach the tissue as close to the nose as possible. |
| | 6. After the participant attaches the tissue to the poster, remove blindfold. |
| | 7. Continue Steps 4-7 until each participant has had a turn. |
| | 8. The participant who places the tissue the closest to the nose wins. |

## Needed Materials:

☐ Instructional Materials and Supports:

"Pin the Tissue on the Nose Poster" (1 Copy – color, laminate, and hang on wall)

☐ Tissues (1 per participant)

☐ Tape

☐ Blindfold

☐ Pencils

☐ Binders

☐ Picking – Lesson Plan 4

**Pin the Tissue on the Nose Poster**

# Picking Activity #9
# "Finger vs. Tissue"

## Instructions:

|   |   |
|---|---|
| 1. | Prior to the start of the game, give each participant 2 voting cards: 1 " Use Tissue Card" and 1 "Finger Is O.K. Card." |
| 2. | Show the participants a picture of an environment. |
| 3. | Have participants determine if the environment is one that requires the use of a tissue to remain socially O.K., or if it is an environment where one could use a finger. Once they determine the answer, Finger vs. Tissue, direct them to vote by raising the corresponding voting card. |
| 4. | The first participant to have the correct answer in the air wins 1 point. |
| 5. | Continue the game, keeping track of each participant's points. |
| 6. | At the conclusion of the game, award prizes to the high point earner(s). |

## Needed Materials:

☐ Instructional Materials and Supports:

"Finger vs. Tissue Voting Cards" (1 "Finger Is O.K. Card" and 1 "Use Tissue Card" per participant)

☐ 10-15 pictures of various environment frequented by participants (bedroom, classroom, restaurant, cafeteria, home bathroom, public bathroom, etc.). These can be actual pictures taken in each environment or pictures found on the Internet or in magazines that represent these places. Cut and paste pictures of each environment on construction paper or other firm paper. Label each card to specify environment. Laminate cards, if desired

☐ Prize for winner(s)

☐ Pencils

☐ Binders

☐ Picking – Lesson Plan 4

# Finger vs. Tissue Voting Cards

**Leader's Instructions:** Cut out each card following the bold line. Glue onto construction paper or other firm paper. Laminate cards. Use for Picking Activity #9 – "Finger vs. Tissue."

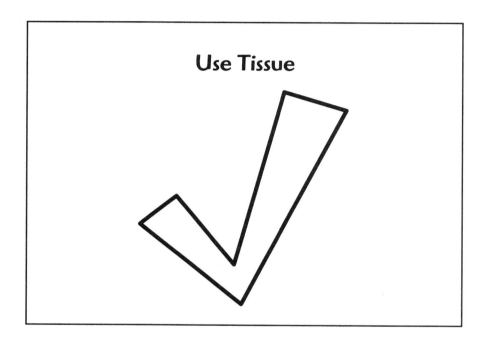

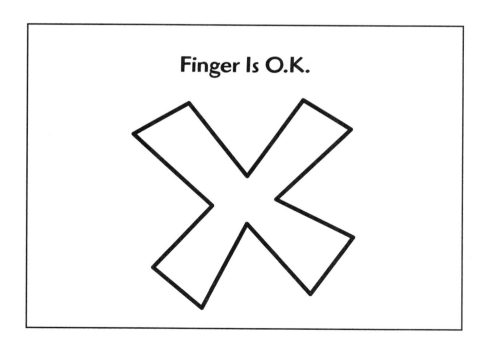

# Picking – Lesson Plan 5

## Session Schedule to Post:

- Chat and review
- Game
- Wrap-up game
- Closing (snack, reward, etc.)

## Lesson Details:

| Estimated Time | Activity or Game | Refer to Pages: |
|---|---|---|
| 5 minutes | 1. Opening – Gather participants. Post and review schedule for session | |
| 5 minutes | 2. REVIEW – Encourage participants to recall Picking Activity #9 – "Finger vs. Tissue." Review the unwritten social rules surrounding this topic | |
| 20 minutes | 3. Picking Activity #10 – "Reaction Time" | 112–114 |
| 10 minutes | 4. Picking Activity #11 – "Picking Wrap-Up" | 115–116 |
| 5 minutes | 5. Closing | |

## Needed Materials:

☐ Instructional Materials and Supports:

"Picking Voting Cards" (1 "Socially O.K. Picking Card" and 1 "Socially Inappropriate Picking Card" per participant)

"Game Cards – Dealing with Picking" (1 copy – cut, glued on firm paper, and laminated)

"Picking Wrap-Up Questions" (1 copy – cut, glued on firm paper, and laminated)

☐ Grand prize for Picking Activity #11 – "Picking Wrap-Up" (1 per participant)

☐ Pencils

☐ Binders

## Following Session, Add to Binder:

Not applicable

# Picking Game #10
# "Reaction Time"

## Instructions:

| | |
|---|---|
| | 1. Prior to the start of the game, place all game cards face down on table. |
| | 2. Pass out the "Picking Voting Cards" to participants. Each participant should have 1 "Socially O.K. Picking Card" and 1 "Socially Inappropriate Picking Card." |
| | 3. Instruct the first participant to select one game card and read it aloud to the group. Then, the participant must either role-play or verbally describe the action he would take in the given situation. Encourage the participant to explain why he would take that action. Ensure that the members are choosing socially appropriate solutions and that they are connecting their solutions to the thoughts and feelings of other people. |
| | 4. Using the Voting Cards, have the remaining participants vote on the participant's solution, determining if it is a socially O.K. or socially inappropriate action. Ask the remaining participants to explain their votes. |
| | 5. Repeat Steps 3-4, switching participants, until all game cards have been used. |

## Needed Materials:

☐ Instructional Materials and Supports:

"Picking Voting Cards" (1 "Socially O.K. Picking Card" and 1 "Socially Inappropriate Picking Card" per participant)

"Game Cards – Dealing with Picking" (1 copy – cut, glued on firm paper, and laminated)

☐ Pencils

☐ Binders

☐ Picking – Lesson Plan 5

# Picking Voting Cards

**Leader's Instructions:** Cut out each card following the bold line. Glue onto construction paper or other firm paper. Laminate cards. Use for Picking Activity #10 – "Reaction Time."

## Socially O.K. Picking

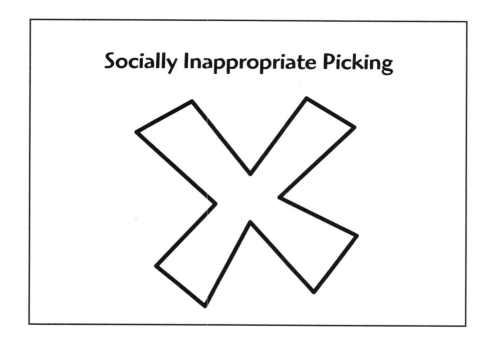

## Socially Inappropriate Picking

# Reaction Time Game Cards – Dealing with Picking

**Leader's Instructions:** Copy this page. Cut cards on the dotted line. Paste on construction paper or other firm paper and laminate (optional). Use cards to play Picking Activity #10 – "Reaction Time."

| | |
|---|---|
| You are eating lunch with several of your classmates and your nose starts to run. | During class, you feel a boogie in your nose. |
| You are eating at a busy restaurant and you feel something in one of the teeth in the back of your mouth. | You are hanging out alone in your bedroom and you feel a boogie in your nose. |
| You are waiting in line at the grocery store and the person in front of you starts picking his nose. | You are talking to your crush and your scab starts to itch. |
| You are in the bathroom at school looking in the mirror and you notice a huge pimple that needs popped. | Your teacher is helping you with your math assignment and you notice that she has a piece of food stuck in her teeth. |
| You are hanging out with your best friend at your house and you notice that she has a piece of food stuck in her teeth. | During a kickball game in gym class, your underwear starts to ride up and gives you a huge wedgie. There are lots of classmates around. |

# Picking Activity #11
# "Picking Wrap-Up"

## Instructions:

| | | |
|---|---|---|
| | 1. | Before the start of the game, spread cards face down on table. |
| | 2. | Explain to participants that the objective of the game is for them to earn at least 6 points. If the participant or group of participants earns at least 6 points collectively, they earn a grand prize. |
| | 3. | To start the game, have a participant choose the first card and read it out loud. |
| | 4. | Encourage the participant to answer the question as thoroughly and accurately as possible. |
| | 5. | Award 1 point if answered correctly. |
| | 6. | Repeat Steps 3-5 until all cards have been used. |
| | 7. | Pass out a grand prize if the participant or group of participants earned 6 points. |

## Needed Materials:

☐ Instructional Materials and Supports:

"Picking Wrap-Up Questions" (1 copy -- cut, pasted on firm paper, and laminated)

☐ Grand prizes

☐ Pencils

☐ Binders

☐ Picking – Lesson Plan 5

# Picking Wrap-Up Questions

**Leader's Instructions:** Cut out each question. Glue onto construction paper or other firm paper. Laminate cards. Use for Picking Activity #11 – "Picking Wrap-Up."

1. What areas of the body do people commonly pick?

2. What do you think about someone when he uses a tissue to blow his nose?

3. What do you think about someone when she picks her nose with her finger?

4. What do you think about someone when you see him picking his teeth? How about scabs? Pimples? Fingernails? Wedgie?

5. What do others think of you when you use a tissue to blow your nose?

6. What do others think of you when you pick your nose? How about scabs? Pimples? Fingernails? Wedgie?

7. When is it socially O.K. to pick your nose, teeth, acne, fingernails, wedgie, or scabs?

# Chapter 5

# Farting and Burping

## Chapter Objectives:

- To understand the written social rules regarding farting and burping.
- To understand the connection between farting and burping and the thoughts and feelings of others.

# List of Activities

The following is a list of activities included in this chapter. Please refer to the subsequent pages for a complete description of each.

1. Introduction to Farting and Burping – Questions

2. Introduction to Farting and Burping – Discussion Guide

3. Movie Clips

4. Fun Farting and Burping Trivia

5. I Can Read Your Mind

6. Farting and Burping Poster

7. People and Places – The Ins and Outs of Farting and Burping

8. "Let 'er Rip?"

9. Emergency Procedures for Farting and Burping

10. Reaction Time

11. Farting and Burping Wrap-Up

# List of Instruction Materials and Supports

The following is a list of instructional materials and supports that may be used to enhance the activities and lessons in this chapter. Please refer to the subsequent pages for a copy of each.

1.  Introduction to Farting and Burping – Questions

2.  Introduction to Farting and Burping – Discussion Guide

3.  Fun Farting and Burping Trivia

4.  Fun Farting and Burping Trivia – Answer Page

5.  Farting and Burping Thought Bubble Worksheet

6.  The Ins and Out of Farting and Burping – Places

7.  The Ins and Out of Farting and Burping – People

8.  Emergency Procedures for Farting and Burping

9.  O.K. vs. Not O.K. Farting and Burping Voting Cards

10. Farting and Burping Voting Cards

11. Reaction Time Game Cards – Dealing with Farting and Burping

14. Farting and Burping Wrap-Up Questions

# Lesson Plan 1 – Farting and Burping

## Session Schedule to Post:

- Chat – introduction to farting and burping
- Movie clips
- Closing (snack, reward, etc.)

## Lesson Details:

| Estimated Time | Activity | Refer to Pages: |
|---|---|---|
| 5 minutes | Opening – Gather participants. Post and review schedule for session | |
| 10 minutes | Farting and Burping Activity #1 – "Introduction to Farting and Burping – Questions" | 121–122 |
| 10 minutes | Farting and Burping Activity #2 – "Introduction to Farting and Burping – Discussion Guide" to facilitate further discussion and provide any missed information | 123–124 |
| 15 minutes | Farting and Burping Activity #3 – "Movie Clips" | 125 |
| 5 minutes | Closing | |

## Needed Materials:

☐ Instructional Materials and Supports:

"Introduction to Farting and Burping – Questions" (1 copy per participant)

"Introduction to Farting and Burping – Discussion Guide" (1 copy per participant)

☐ Video clips of people farting and burping (2 clips per participant). Please refer to the References and Other Resources for tips regarding movie clips

☐ Computer or other means of playing movie clips

☐ Pencils

☐ Binders

## Following Session, Add to Binder:

☐ "Introduction to Farting and Burping – Questions" – completed version

☐ "Introduction to Farting and Burping – Discussion Guide"

# Farting and Burping Activity #1
# "Introduction to Farting and Burping – Questions"

## Instructions:

|  | 1. | Give each participant a copy of "Introduction to Farting – Questions." |
|---|---|---|
|  | 2. | Instruct participants to write answers to the questions on their worksheet. If writing is a source of anxiety or frustration, offer accommodations (scribe, partner with another participant, etc.). |
|  | 3. | Set timer for a designated time period, if needed. |
|  | 4. | When participants are finished, read the first question aloud to the group. |
|  | 5. | Have participants share their answers. Discuss. |
|  | 6. | Repeat Steps 4–5 until each question has been discussed. |

## Needed Materials:

☐ Instructional Materials and Supports:

"Introduction to Farting and Burping – Questions" (1 copy per participant)

☐ Pencils

☐ Binders

☐ Farting and Burping – Lesson Plan 1

# Introduction to Farting and Burping – Questions

**Instructions:** After reading the question, write your answers in the space provided.

What does it mean to have socially O.K. farting and burping habits?

How do your farting and burping behaviors impact the thoughts and feelings of other people?

What social rules regarding farting and burping are important to follow if you want to make a good impression?

1.

2.

3.

4.

5.

6.

# Farting and Burping Activity #2
# "Introduction to Farting and Burping – Discussion Guide"

## Instructions:

| | |
|---|---|
| | 1. Give each participant a copy of "Introduction to Farting and Burping – Discussion Guide." |
| | 2. Read the first question out loud. |
| | 3. Choose a participant to answer the question by reading the information provided on the worksheet or by expanding on the information on the worksheet. |
| | 4. Challenge the other participants to think of additional information that is not provided on the worksheet. |
| | 5. Repeat Steps 2-4 until all of the questions are discussed. |

## Needed Materials:

☐ Instructional Materials and Supports:

"Introduction to Farting and Burping – Discussion Guide" (1 copy per participant)

☐ Pencils

☐ Binders

☐ Farting and Burping – Lesson Plan 1

# Introduction to Farting and Burping – Discussion Guide

### What does it mean to have socially O.K. farting and burping habits?

Assessing where you are and who you are with to determine if it is socially O.K. to burp out loud or fart.

### How do your farting and burping behaviors impact the thoughts and feelings of other people?

If you have socially O.K. farting and burping habits, others will think more positively about you. If you have inappropriate farting and burping habits, others will think gross thoughts about you and will most likely not want to interact with you.

### What social rules regarding farting and burping are important to remember if you want to make a good impression?

1. It is only O.K. to burp loudly if you are in the company of people that you know really well.

2. It is only O.K. to fart if you are in the company of people that you know really well.

3. If you need to burp, burp quietly and say, "excuse me."

4. If you need to fart, go to another area, away from others.

5. If you smell a fart, ignore it.

6. If you hear someone fart, ignore it.

# Farting and Burping Activity #3
## "Movie Clips"

## Instructions:

|  | |
|---|---|
| | 1. Start the activity by showing the first movie clip. Carefully note each participant's reaction, to be used during upcoming discussion. |
| | 2. Have participants share their impressions of the person in the video clip. Use the following questions to guide the discussion:<br>• What was your initial reaction to the person's behavior? (use observations from Step 1 for reinforcement)<br>• What were you thinking about that person and his behavior?<br>• What were other people in the clip thinking about the person who was farting and burping? |
| | 3. Continue Steps 1–2 until participants have viewed all clips. |
| | 4. After watching all of the clips, discuss the prevalence of farting and burping clips on the Internet or in movies. Discuss how the clips are often included for the purpose of inserting humor and that many people find the clips funny. It is important to stress that it becomes much different when the farting and burping behaviors occur during a real-life situation. Encourage participants to determine the difference between farting and burping behaviors in a movie and in real life. To guide the discussion, use the following questions:<br>• Why are these clips so prevalent?<br>• Do a lot of people find the clips funny?<br>• What is the difference between the people in the clips and real-life situations?<br>• When is it funny to fart or burp in real life?<br>• When is it NOT funny to fart or burp in real life? |

## Needed Materials:

☐ Movie clips of people demonstrating farting and burping behaviors (download from Internet or find in various movies). Please refer to the References and Other Resources for tips regarding movie clips

☐ Computer or other means of playing video clips

☐ Binders

☐ Farting and Burping – Lesson Plan 1

# Lesson Plan 2 – Farting and Burping

## Session Schedule to Post:

- Chat and review
- Fun trivia
- Fun activity
- Closing (snack, reward, etc.)

## Lesson Details:

| Estimated Time | Activity | Refer to Pages: |
|---|---|---|
| 5 minutes | Opening – Gather participants. Post and review schedule for session | |
| 5 minutes | REVIEW – Have participants briefly recall the information covered the previous session. If needed, refer them to the following forms added to their binders: "Introduction to Farting and Burping – Questions" and "Introduction to Farting and Burping – Discussion Guide" | |
| 10 minutes | Farting and Burping Activity #4 – "Fun Farting and Burping Trivia" | 127–129 |
| 20 minutes | Farting and Burping Activity #5 – "I Can Read Your Mind" | 130–131 |
| 5 minutes | Closing | |

## Needed Materials:

- ☐ Instructional Materials and Supports:
  "Farting and Burping Thought Bubble Worksheet" (2 copies per participants)
- ☐ 1 copy of "Fun Farting and Burping Trivia," cut and pasted on index cards
- ☐ 1 copy of "Fun Farting and Burping Trivia – Answer Page"
- ☐ Pictures of people/cartoons demonstrating socially O.K. or socially inappropriate behaviors revolving around farting and burping (1-2 pictures per participant) OR movie clips used during Farting and Burping Activity #3 (1-2 movie clips per participant). Please refer to the References and Other Resources for tips on finding pictures and movie clips
- ☐ Computer or other means of playing video clips (if using movie clips for Farting and Burping Activity #5)
- ☐ Pencils
- ☐ Markers
- ☐ Scissors
- ☐ Glue
- ☐ Binders

## Following Session, Add to Binder:

- ☐ "Farting and Burping Thought Bubble Worksheet" – completed version

# Farting and Burping Activity #4
# "Fun Farting and Burping Trivia"

## Instructions:

| | |
|---|---|
| | 1. Spread the index cards face down on table or floor. |
| | 2. Have the first participant pick a card and read the trivia question out loud to the rest of the group. |
| | 3. Encourage the reader to answer the question or share his best guess. |
| | 4. Challenge each of the other participants to also guess the answer. |
| | 5. After each participant has had a turn to guess, read the correct answer out loud. |
| | 6. Repeat Steps 2-5 until all of the trivia questions have been discussed. |

## Needed Materials:

☐ 1 copy of "Fun Farting and Burping Trivia," cut, pasted on index cards, and laminated

☐ 1 copy of "Fun Farting and Burping Trivia – Answer Page"

☐ Binders

☐ Farting and Burping – Lesson Plan 2

# Fun Farting and Burping Trivia

**Leader's Instructions:** Cut and paste each question on a separate index card. Laminate, if desired. Use for Farting and Burping Activity #4 – "Fun Farting and Burping Trivia."

Q: Does everyone fart and burp?

Q: How many times a day do most people fart and burp?

Q: What causes burps?

Q: What causes farts?

Q: Where does the gas in our intestines come from?

Q: How long does it take a fart to travel through your body?

Q: What animal is thought to fart the most frequently?

# Fun Farting and Burping Trivia – Answer Page

*Adapted from www.heptune.com/farts.html and www.kidshealth.org*

**Q: Does everyone fart and burp?**

A:   *Yes. Everyone farts and burps.*

**Q: How many times a day do most people fart and burp?**

A:   *Research has found that people fart or burp an average of 14 times a day.*

**Q: What causes burps?**

A:   *When we eat, we swallow a lot of air. This air eventually leaves our stomach and comes out of our bodies as burps.*

**Q: What causes farts?**

A:   *Farts are caused by gases released from our intestines.*

**Q: Where does the gas in our intestines come from?**

A:   *Intestinal gas comes from several sources: the air we swallow, gas that seeps into our intestines from our blood, gas produced by chemical reactions in our intestines, and gas produced by bacteria living in our guts.*

**Q: How long does it take a fart to travel through your body?**

A:   *30–45 minutes.*

**Q: What animal is thought to fart the most frequently?**

A:   *Termites. Because of their diet and digestive process, they produce as much methane gas as industrial factories.  In fact, termite farts are believed to be a major contributor to global warming.*

# Farting and Burping Activity #5
## "I Can Read Your Mind"

## Instructions:

| | | |
|---|---|---|
| ☐ | 1. | Have participants cut and glue the first picture OR have them draw/write a description of the first movie clip assigned on a "Farting and Burping Hygiene Thought Bubble Worksheet." |
| ☐ | 2. | Instruct participants to begin completing the first "Farting and Burping Thought Bubble Worksheet" by determining if the picture is an example of socially O.K. or socially inappropriate farting and burping. |
| ☐ | 3. | To complete the first "Farting and Burping Thought Bubble Worksheet," encourage participants to list the common thoughts and feelings the other person would have, based on the farting or burping behavior of the person in the picture. Have them write their answers in the blank thought bubble provided. You may need to support participants if they are having difficulty. For example, you can write a list of potential thoughts and feelings on the board and have participants select from that list (to add difficulty provide some correct answers and some answers that are incorrect). |
| ☐ | 4. | To complete the assignment, instruct participants to repeat Steps 1–3 using the second picture OR movie clip. |
| ☐ | 5. | When everyone is finished, have each participant share the end product with the group. |

## Needed Materials:

☐ Instructional Materials and Supports:

"Farting and Burping Thought Bubble Worksheet" (2 copies per participant)

☐ Pictures of people/cartoons demonstrating socially O.K. or socially inappropriate behaviors revolving around farting and burping OR movie clips used during Farting and Burping Activity #3 – "Movie Clips." Please refer to the References of Other Resources for tips on finding pictures and movie clips (2 pictures or movie clips per participant)

☐ Computer or other means of playing video clips

☐ Scissors

☐ Glue

☐ Pencils

☐ Binders

# Farting and Burping Thought Bubble Worksheet

## Instructions:

1. Attach a picture in the designated area.
2. Determine if the person in the picture demonstrates socially O.K. farting or burping or socially inappropriate farting or burping by circling the corresponding answer in the area below.
3. Based on the farting or burping behavior of the person in the picture, list the common thoughts and feelings the other person might have in the blank thought bubble provided.

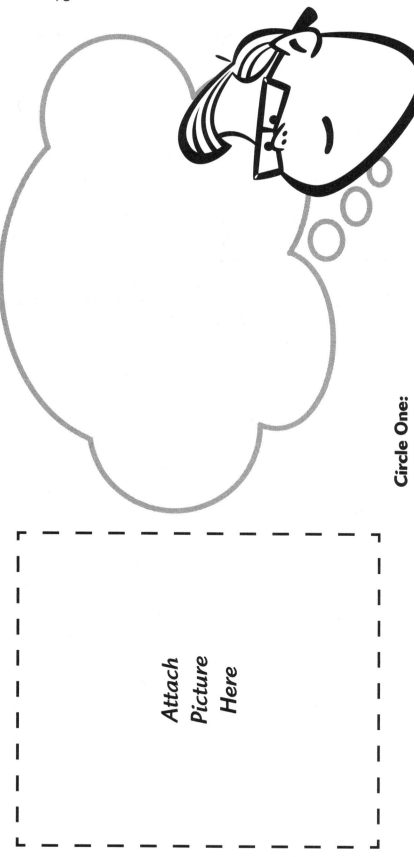

Attach
Picture
Here

**Circle One:**

Socially O.K. Farting and Burping          Socially Inappropriate Farting and Burping

# Lesson Plan 3 – Farting and Burping

## Session Schedule to Post:

- Chat and review
- Fun activity – poster
- Brainstorming session
- Closing (snack, reward, etc.)

## Lesson Details:

| Estimated Time | Activity | Refer to Pages: |
|---|---|---|
| 5 minutes | Opening – Gather participants. Post and review schedule for session | |
| 5 minutes | REVIEW – Have group review their "Farting and Burping Thought Bubble Worksheets" from previous session | |
| 10 minutes | Farting and Burping Activity #6 – "Farting and Burping Poster" | 133 |
| 20 minutes | Farting and Burping Activity #7 – "People and Places – The Ins and Outs of Farting and Burping" | 134-136 |
| 5 minutes | Closing | |

## Needed Materials:

☐ Instructional Materials and Supports:
   "The Ins and Outs of Farting and Burping – Places" (1 copy per participant)
   "The Ins and Outs of Farting and Burping – People" (1 copy per participant)
☐ "Farting and Burping Thought Bubble Worksheet" completed during previous session
☐ *Optional:* Copies of all completed "Oral Hygiene Thought Bubble Worksheets" (so participants can keep originals in their binders)
☐ Pencils
☐ Scissors
☐ Glue
☐ Markers
☐ Poster board or other large piece of paper (for Farting and Burping Activity #6)
☐ 2 large pieces of paper divided in half by drawing a line down the center. On the first piece of paper, label one side "Socially O.K. Places" and the second side, "Socially Inappropriate Places." On the second piece of paper, label one side "Socially O.K. People" and the other side, "Socially Inappropriate People"
☐ Binders

## Following Session, Add to Binder:

☐ "People and Places – The Ins and Outs of Farting and Burping" – completed version

# Farting and Burping Activity #6
# "Farting and Burping Poster"

## Instructions:

| | |
|---|---|
| 1. | Gather the completed "Farting and Burping Hygiene Thought Bubble Worksheets" from Farting and Burping Activity #5 – "I Can Read Your Mind." |
| 2. | *Optional:* Copy each page so participants can keep originals in their binders. |
| 3. | Instruct the participants to attach the completed "Farting and Burping Thought Bubble Worksheets" on a poster board or other large piece of paper. |
| 4. | Display poster in a central area for quick referral. |

## Needed Materials:

☐ Completed "Farting and Burping Thought Bubble Worksheets"

☐ *Optional:* Copies of all completed "Farting and Burping Thought Bubble Worksheets" (so participants can keep originals in their binders)

☐ Markers

☐ Glue

☐ Scissors

☐ Poster board or large piece of paper

☐ Pencils

☐ Binders

☐ Farting and Burping – Lesson Plan 3

# Farting and Burping Activity #7
# "People and Places – The Ins and Outs of Farting and Burping"

## Instructions:

| | |
|---|---|
| | 1. Before the start of the activity, position participants so that everyone can see the large piece of paper (hang on wall for easiest viewing). |
| | 2. Give each participant a copy of "People and Places – The Ins and Outs of Farting and Burping." Instruct them to follow along with the activity and write answers in the appropriate sections. |
| | 3. Introduce the activity using the following discussion questions:<br>• Are there situations where farting and burping are considered socially O.K.? How do you determine if it is socially O.K.?<br>• Are there situations where farting and burping are considered socially inappropriate? How do you determine if it is socially inappropriate? |
| | 4. Start the brainstorming session by asking participants to list places where it is considered socially O.K. to fart. Also, have them list places where it is considered socially O.K. to burp. Write the answers in the designated section on the large paper. |
| | 5. Remind participants to write answers on their worksheets. |
| | 6. Ask participants to brainstorm places where it is socially inappropriate to fart. Also, have them list places where it is considered socially inappropriate to burp. Write the answers in the designated section on the large paper. |
| | 7. Remind participants to write answers on their worksheets. |
| | 8. Repeat Steps 4-7, brainstorming people around whom it is socially O.K. and socially inappropriate to fart and burp. |

## Needed Materials:

☐ Instructional Materials and Supports:
   "The Ins and Outs of Farting and Burping – Places" (1 copy per participant)
   "The Ins and Outs of Farting and Burping – People" (1 copy per participant)
☐ Markers
☐ 2 large pieces of paper, each divided in half by drawing a line down the center. On the first piece of paper, label one side "Socially O.K. Places" and the other, "Socially Inappropriate Places." On the second piece of paper, label one side "Socially O.K. People" and the other, "Socially Inappropriate People"
☐ Tape to hang paper
☐ Pencils
☐ Binders
☐ Farting and Burping – Lesson Plan 3

# The Ins and Outs of Farting and Burping – Places

**Instructions:** Write answers generated from Picking Activity #7 – "People and Places – The Ins and Outs of Farting and Burping" in the spaces provided below.

| Socially O.K. Places | Socially Inappropriate Places |
|---|---|
| 1. | 1. |
| 2. | 2. |
| 3. | 3. |
| 4. | 4. |
| 5. | 5. |
| 6. | 6. |
| 7. | 7. |
| 8. | 8. |

# The Ins and Outs of Farting and Burping – People

**Instructions:** Write answers generated from Picking Activity #7 – "People and Places – The Ins and Outs of Farting and Burping" in the spaces provided below.

| Socially O.K. People | Socially Inappropriate People |
|---|---|
| 1. | 1. |
| 2. | 2. |
| 3. | 3. |
| 4. | 4. |
| 5. | 5. |
| 6. | 6. |
| 7. | 7. |
| 8. | 8. |

# Lesson Plan 4 – Farting and Burping

## Session Schedule to Post:

- Chat and review
- Game
- Discussion
- Closing (snack, reward, etc.)

## Lesson Details:

| Estimated Time | Activity | Refer to Pages: |
|---|---|---|
| 5 minutes | Opening – Gather participants. Post and review schedule for session | |
| 5 minutes | REVIEW – Review posters on display created during Farting and Burping Activity #7 "People and Places – A Brainstorming Session" from previous session | |
| 15 minutes | Farting and Burping Activity #8 – "Let 'er Rip?" | 138–139 |
| 15 minutes | Farting and Burping Activity #9 – "Emergency Procedures for Farting and Burping" | 140–141 |
| 5 minutes | Closing | |

## Needed Materials:

☐ Instructional Materials and Supports:

"O.K. vs. Inappropriate Farting and Burping Voting Cards" (1 "Socially O.K. to Fart and Burp Card" and 1 "NOT O.K. to Fart and Burp Card" per participant)

"Emergency Procedures for Farting and Burping" (1 copy per participant)

☐ Easy view of posters created during Farting and Burping Activity #7 from previous session

☐ 10-15 pictures of various environments frequented by participants, glued on firm paper and labeled to specify environment pictured. These can be actual pictures taken in each environment or pictures found on the Internet or in magazines that represent each of these places.

☐ Pencils

☐ Binders

## Following Session, Add to Binder:

☐ "Emergency Procedures for Farting and Burping"

# Farting and Burping Activity #8
## "Let 'er Rip?"

## Instructions:

| | | |
|---|---|---|
| | 1. | Before the start of the game, give each participant 2 voting cards: "O.K. to Fart or Burp Card" and "Not O.K. to Fart or Burp Card." |
| | 2. | Show participants a picture of an environment. |
| | 3. | Have participants determine if the environment is one where it is O.K. or NOT O.K. to fart or burp. Once they determine the answer, O.K. vs. NOT O.K., have them vote by raising the corresponding voting card. |
| | 4. | The first participant to have the correct answer in the air earns 1 point. |
| | 5. | Continue the game, keeping track of each participant's points. |
| | 6. | At the conclusion of the game, award prizes to the high-point earner(s). |

## Needed Materials:

☐ Instructional Materials and Supports:

"O.K. vs. Inappropriate Farting and Burping Voting Cards" (1 "Socially O.K. to Fart and Burp Card" and 1 "Socially Inappropriate to Fart or Burp Card" per participant)

☐ 10-15 pictures of various environments frequented by participants (bedroom, classroom, restaurant, cafeteria, home bathroom, public bathroom, etc.). These can be actual pictures taken in each environment or pictures found on the Internet or in magazines that represent each of these places. Cut and paste photos of each environment on construction paper or other firm paper. Label each card to specify environment. Laminate cards, if desired

☐ Prize for winner(s)

☐ Pencils

☐ Binders

# O.K. vs. Inappropriate Farting and Burping Voting Cards

**Leader's Instructions:** Cut out each card following the bold line. Glue onto construction paper or other firm paper. Laminate cards. Use for Farting and Burping Activity #8 – "Let 'er Rip?"

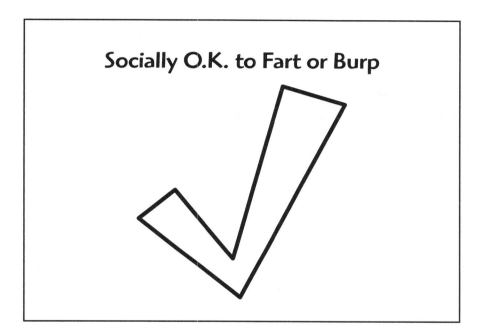

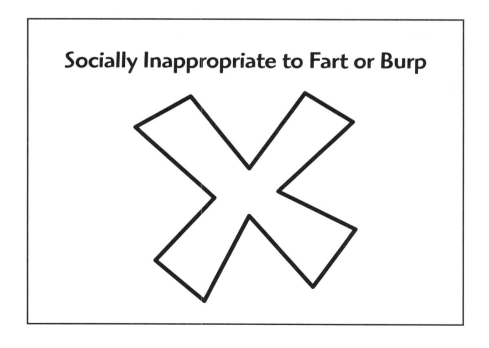

# Farting and Burping Activity #9
# "Emergency Procedures for Farting and Burping"

## Instructions:

| | |
|---|---|
| | 1. To start activity, give each participant a copy of "Emergency Procedure for Farting and Burping." |
| | 2. Using this resource, lead a discussion about handling common situations surrounding farting or burping. Discuss typical things to consider and typical methods of handling socially embarrassing situations. |
| | 3. As the discussion proceeds, ask participants to add any relevant information that may not have been provided on the worksheet. |

## Needed Materials:

☐ Instructional Materials and Supports:

"Emergency Procedures for Farting and Burping" (1 copy per participant)

☐ Pencils

☐ Binders

☐ Farting and Burping – Lesson Plan 4

# Emergency Procedures for Farting and Burping

| Situation | Things to Consider | Emergency Procedures |
|---|---|---|
| You have an urge to fart | • Where are you?<br>• Who is around?<br>• Any chance of getting caught? | • Let it go freely<br>• Let it go quietly; ignore it<br>• Go to another area<br>• Hold it in |
| You have an urge to burp | • Where are you?<br>• Who is around?<br>• Any chance of getting caught? | • Let it go freely<br>• Let it go quietly; say, "Excuse me"<br>• Go to another area |
| You accidentally fart | • Where are you?<br>• Who is around?<br>• Any chance of getting caught? | • Ignore it<br>• Move to another area quickly<br>• If someone catches you, laugh; say, "Excuse Me"; or ignore the comment |
| You accidentally burp loudly | • Where are you?<br>• Who is around?<br>• Any chance of getting caught? | • Say, "Excuse me"<br>• Ignore it<br>• Laugh |
| You hear another person fart | • Who is the person?<br>• How well do you know the person?<br>• What sense of humor does that person have?<br>• Where are you?<br>• Are other people around? | • Ignore it<br>• Laugh |
| You smell a fart | • Where are you?<br>• Who is close by?<br>• How well do you know the people close by? | • Ignore it<br>• Laugh |
| You hear someone burp | • Who is the person?<br>• How well do you know the person?<br>• What sense of humor does that person have?<br>• Where are you?<br>• Are other people around? | • Ignore it<br>• Laugh |

# Lesson Plan 5 – Farting and Burping

## Session Schedule to Post:

- Chat and review
- Game
- Wrap-up game
- Closing (snack, reward, etc.)

## Lesson Details:

| Estimated Time | Activity | Refer to Pages: |
|---|---|---|
| 5 minutes | Opening – Gather participants. Post and review schedule for session | |
| 5 minutes | REVIEW – Using the "Emergency Procedures for Farting and Burping," review the typical ways to handle common situations involving farting and burping | |
| 20 minutes | Farting and Burping Activity #10 – "Reaction Time" | 143-145 |
| 10 minutes | Farting and Burping Activity #11 – "Farting and Burping Wrap-Up" | 146-147 |
| 5 minutes | Closing | |

## Needed Materials:

☐ Instructional Materials and Supports:
"Farting and Burping Voting Cards" (1 "Socially O.K. to Fart or Burp Card" and 1 "Socially Inappropriate to Fart or Burp Card" per participant)
"Reaction Time Game Cards" (1 copy – cut, glued on firm paper, and laminated)
"Farting and Burping Wrap-Up Questions" (1 copy – cut, glued on firm paper, and laminated)
☐ "Emergency Procedures for Farting and Burping" (completed version from previous session)
☐ Grand prizes for Farting and Burping Activity #11 – "Farting and Burping Wrap-Up"
☐ Pencils
☐ Binders

## Following Session, Add to Binder:

Not applicable

# Farting and Burping Activity #10
## "Reaction Time"

## Instructions:

| | | |
|---|---|---|
| | 1. | Prior to the start of the game, place all game cards face down on table. |
| | 2. | Pass out the "Farting and Burping Voting Cards." Each participant should have 1 "Socially O.K. Farting and Burping Card" and 1 "Socially Inappropriate Farting and Burping Card." |
| | 3. | Instruct the first participant to select one game card and read it out loud to the group. Then, the participant must either role-play or verbally describe the action she would take in the given situation. Encourage her to explain why she would take that action. Ensure that the members are choosing socially appropriate solutions and that they are connecting their solutions to the thoughts and feelings of other people. |
| | 4. | Using the voting cards, have the remaining group members vote on the participant's solution, determining if it is a socially O.K. or socially inappropriate action. Ask remaining participants to explain their votes. |
| | 5. | Repeat Steps 3-4, switching participants, until all game cards have been used. |

## Needed Materials:

☐ Instructional Materials and Supports:

"Farting and Burping Voting Cards" (1 "Socially O.K. to Fart or Burp Card" and 1 "Socially Inappropriate to Fart or Burp Card" per participant)

"Game Cards – Dealing with Farting and Burping" (1 copy – cut, glued on firm paper, and laminated)

☐ Pencils

☐ Binders

☐ Farting and Burping – Lesson Plan 5

# Farting and Burping Voting Cards

**Leader's Instructions:** Cut out each card following the bold line. Glue onto construction paper or other firm paper. Laminate cards. Use for Farting and Burping Activity #10 – "Reaction Time."

# Reaction Time Game Cards
# Dealing with Farting and Burping

**Leader's Instructions:** Copy this page. Cut cards along the dotted line. Paste on construction paper or other firm paper and laminate (optional). Use cards to play Farting and Burping Activity #10 – "Reaction Time."

| | |
|---|---|
| You are eating lunch with several of your classmates and you accidentally burp loudly. | During class, you have an urge to fart. |
| You are eating at a busy restaurant and you have an urge to burp. | You are hanging out at your house with your best friend and you have an urge to burp. |
| You are waiting in line at the grocery store and the person in front of you farts loudly. | You are talking to your crush and you have an urge to fart. |
| You are in the bathroom at school and you have an urge to fart. | Your teacher is helping you with your math assignment and you smell a fart. |
| You are hanging out with your best friend at your house and you smell a fart. | You are talking to your crush and you accidentally burp loudly. |

# Farting and Burping Activity #11
# "Farting and Burping Wrap-Up"

## Instructions:

| | | |
|---|---|---|
| | 1. | Before the start of the game, spread cards face down on table. |
| | 2. | Explain to participants that the objective of the game is for them to earn at least 6 points. If at least 6 points are earned by the participant or collectively by a group of participants, they earn a grand prize. |
| | 3. | To start the game, have a participant choose a card and read it out loud. |
| | 4. | Encourage the participant to answer the question as thoroughly and accurately as possible. |
| | 5. | Award 1 point if answered correctly. |
| | 6. | Repeat Steps 3-6 until all cards have been used. |
| | 7. | Pass out a grand prize if 6 points were earned by the participant or the group. |

## Needed Materials:

☐ Instructional Materials and Supports:

"Farting and Burping Wrap-Up Questions" (1 copy – cut, pasted on firm paper, and laminated)

☐ Grand prizes

☐ Pencils

☐ Binders

☐ Farting and Burping – Lesson Plan 5

# Farting and Burping Wrap-Up Questions

**Leader's Instructions:** Cut out each question. Glue onto construction paper or other firm paper. Laminate cards. Use for Farting and Burping Activity #11 – "Farting and Burping Wrap-Up."

1. Is it O.K to fart and burp?

2. What are important things to think about if you have to fart or burp?

3. Where is it O.K. to fart?

4. Where is it O.K. to burp?

5. Who is it O.K. to fart and burp in front of?

6. What do you think about someone who farts in front of you?

7. What do you think about someone who burps in front of you?

8. How should you react if someone farts or burps in front of you?

9. What do others think of you if you fart or burp around them?

# Chapter 6

# General Bathroom Hygiene and Using Public Restrooms

## Chapter Objectives:

- To establish basic knowledge of good hygiene practices in the bathroom.
- To understand the connection between personal hygiene and the thoughts and feelings of others.
- To understand the unwritten social rules of a public restroom.

# List of Activities

The following is a list of activities included in this chapter. Please refer to the subsequent pages for a complete description of each.

1. Introduction to Bathroom Hygiene – Questions

2. Introduction to Bathroom Hygiene – Discussion Guide

3. Movie Clips

4. Fun Bathroom Hygiene Trivia

5. I Can Read Your Mind

6. Bathroom Hygiene Poster

7. The Social Rules of a Public Restroom

8. The Urinal Game

9. Every Vote Counts

10. Reaction Time

11. Bathroom Hygiene Wrap-up

# List of Instructional Materials and Supports

The following is a list of instructional materials and supports that may be used to enhance the activities and lessons in this chapter. Please refer to the subsequent pages for a copy of each.

1. Introduction to Bathroom Hygiene – Questions

2. Introduction to Bathroom Hygiene – Discussion Guide

3. Fun Bathroom Hygiene Trivia

4. Fun Bathroom Hygiene Trivia – Answer Page

5. Bathroom Hygiene Thought Bubble Worksheet

6. The Social Rules of a Public Restroom

7. Number Cards for Urinal Game

8. Scenario Cards for Urinal Game

9. Bathroom Behavior Voting Cards 1

10. Bathroom Behavior Voting Cards 2

11. Reaction Time Game Cards – Bathroom Behaviors

12. Bathroom Hygiene Wrap-Up Questions

# Bathroom Hygiene – Lesson Plan 1

## Session Schedule to Post:

- Chat – introduction to bathroom hygiene
- Movie clips
- Closing (snack, reward, etc.)

## Lesson Details:

| Estimated Time | Activity | Refer to Pages: |
|---|---|---|
| 5 minutes | Opening – Gather participants. Post and review schedule for session | |
| 10 minutes | Bathroom Hygiene Activity #1 – "Introduction to Bathroom Hygiene – Questions" | 153–154 |
| 10 minutes | Bathroom Hygiene Activity #2 – "Introduction to Bathroom Hygiene – Discussion Guide" to facilitate further discussion and provide any missed information | 155–156 |
| 15 minutes | Bathroom Hygiene Activity #3 – "Movie Clips" | 157 |
| 5 minutes | Closing | |

## Needed Materials:

☐ Instructional Materials and Supports:

   "Introduction to Bathroom Hygiene – Questions" (1 copy per participant)

   "Introduction to Bathroom Hygiene – Discussion Guide" (1 copy per participant)

☐ Movie clips of people demonstrating bathroom behaviors. Please refer to References and Other Resources for tips regarding movie clips

☐ Computer or other means of playing video clips

☐ Pencils

☐ Binders

## Following Session, Add to Binder:

☐ "Introduction to Bathroom Hygiene – Questions" – completed version

☐ "Introduction to Bathroom Hygiene – Discussion Guide"

# Bathroom Hygiene Activity #1
# "Introduction to Bathroom Hygiene – Questions"

## Instructions:

| | |
|---|---|
| 1. | Give each participant a copy of "Introduction to Bathroom Hygiene – Questions." |
| 2. | Instruct participants to write answers to the questions on their worksheet. If writing is a source of anxiety or frustration, offer accommodations (scribe, partner with another participant, etc.). |
| 3. | Set timer for a designated time period, if needed. |
| 4. | When participants are finished, read the first question aloud to the group. |
| 5. | Have participants share their answers. Discuss. |
| 6. | Repeat Steps 4-5 until each question is discussed. |

## Needed Materials:

☐ Instructional Materials and Supports:

"Introduction to Bathroom Hygiene – Questions" (1 copy per participant)

☐ Pencils

☐ Binders

☐ Bathroom Hygiene – Lesson Plan 1

# Introduction to Bathroom Hygiene – Questions

**Instructions:** After reading the question, write your answer in the space provided.

What does "good bathroom hygiene" mean?

How do bathroom hygiene habits impact the thoughts and feelings of other people?

What tasks should I do to have good bathroom hygiene?

1.

2.

3.

4.

What are some of the social rules in a public bathroom that I need to follow if I want to make a good impression and be safe?

1.

2.

3.

4.

5.

6.

# Bathroom Hygiene Activity #2
# "Introduction to Bathroom Hygiene – Discussion Guide"

## Instructions:

| | | |
|---|---|---|
| | 1. | Give each participant a copy of "Introduction to Bathroom Hygiene – Discussion Guide." |
| | 2. | Read the first question out loud. |
| | 3. | Choose a participant to answer the question by reading the information provided on the worksheet or by expanding on the information on the worksheet. |
| | 4. | Challenge the other participants to think of additional information that is not provided on the worksheet. |
| | 5. | Repeat Steps 2–4 until all of the questions have discussed. |

## Needed Materials:

☐ Instructional Materials and Supports:

"Introduction to Bathroom Hygiene – Discussion Guide" (1 copy per participant)

☐ Pencils

☐ Binders

☐ Bathroom Hygiene – Lesson Plan 1

# Introduction to Bathroom Hygiene – Discussion Guide

### What does "good bathroom hygiene" mean?

Using good strategies to stay clean and avoid germs in the bathroom.

### How do bathroom hygiene habits impact the thoughts and feelings of other people?

If you follow good bathroom hygiene habits, it will help you make a good impression on other people. Using good hygiene habits causes others to have "good" thoughts about you, and using poor hygiene habits causes others to have "weird" or "gross" thoughts about you.

### What tasks should I do to have good bathroom hygiene?

1. Use toilet paper.

2. Flush the toilet (use foot to flush when possible).

3. Wash hands with soap and water. Dry hands well.

4. Touch as little as possible.

### What are some of the social rules in a public bathroom that you need to use if I want to make a good impression and be safe?

1. Avoid eye contact, especially with strangers.

2. If possible, select a stall or urinal that is not next to someone else.

3. Have only one person per stall.

4. For men, avoid small talk when using urinal.

5. For men, keep eyes straight when using urinal (no peeking at neighbors).

6. When standing at a urinal, unzip pants to go to the bathroom. Do not pull pants down around ankles.

# Bathroom Hygiene Activity #3
# "Movie Clips"

## Instructions:

| | |
|---|---|
| | 1. Start activity by showing the first movie clip. Carefully note each participant's reaction, to be used during upcoming discussion. |
| | 2. Have each participant share his impression of the person in the video clip. Use the following questions to guide the discussion:<br>• What was your initial reaction to the person's behavior? (use observations from Step 1 for reinforcement)<br>• What were you thinking about that person and her behavior?<br>• What were other people in the clip thinking about the person who was demonstrating bathroom behaviors? |
| | 3. Continue Steps 1–2 until the participants have viewed all clips. |

## Needed Materials:

☐ Movie clips of people demonstrating bathroom behaviors (download from Internet or find in various movies). Please refer to References and Other Resources for tips regarding movie clips

☐ Computer or other means of playing video clips

☐ Binders

☐ Bathroom Hygiene – Lesson Plan 1

# Bathroom Hygiene – Lesson Plan 2

## Session Schedule to Post:

- Chat and review
- Fun trivia
- Fun activity
- Closing (snack, reward, etc.)

## Lesson Details:

| Estimated Time | Activity | Refer to Pages: |
|---|---|---|
| 5 minutes | Opening – Gather participants. Post and review schedule for session | |
| 5 minutes | REVIEW – Have participants briefly recall the information covered during the previous session. If needed, refer them to the following forms added to the binders: "Introduction to Bathroom Hygiene – Questions" and "Introduction to Bathroom Hygiene – Discussion Guide" | |
| 15 minutes | Bathroom Hygiene Activity #4 – "Fun Bathroom Hygiene Trivia" | 159–161 |
| 15 minutes | Bathroom Hygiene Activity #5 – "I Can Read Your Mind" | 162–163 |
| 5 minutes | Closing | |

## Needed Materials:

☐ Instructional Materials and Supports:
  "Fun Bathroom Hygiene Trivia" (1 copy, cut, pasted on index cards, and laminated)
  "Fun Bathroom Hygiene Trivia – Answer Page" (1 copy)
  "Bathroom Hygiene Thought Bubble Worksheet" (2 copies per participant)
☐ Pictures of people demonstrating a mix of good and poor bathroom hygiene habits (2 pictures per participant)
☐ Pencils
☐ Markers
☐ Scissors
☐ Glue
☐ Binders

## Following Session, Add to Binder:

☐ "Bathroom Hygiene Thought Bubble Worksheets" – completed version

# Bathroom Hygiene Activity #4
# "Fun Bathroom Hygiene Trivia"

## Instructions:

| | |
|---|---|
| | 1. At the start of activity, spread the index cards face down on table or floor. |
| | 2. Have the first participant pick a card and read the trivia question out loud to the rest of the group. |
| | 3. Encourage the reader to answer the question or share her best guess. |
| | 4. Challenge each of the other participants to also guess the answer. |
| | 5. After each participant has had a turn to guess, read the correct answer out loud. |
| | 6. Repeat Steps 2-5 until all of the trivia questions have been discussed. |

## Needed Materials:

☐ 1 copy of "Fun Bathroom Hygiene Trivia" – cut, pasted on index cards, and laminated

☐ 1 copy of "Fun Bathroom Hygiene Trivia – Answer Page"

☐ Binders

☐ Bathroom Hygiene – Lesson Plan 2

# Fun Bathroom Hygiene Trivia

**Leader's Instructions:** Cut and paste each question on a separate index card. Laminate, if desired. Use for Bathroom Hygiene Activity #4 – "Fun Bathroom Hygiene Trivia."

Q:  What percentage of men wash their hands after using the restroom?

Q:  What percentage of women wash their hands after using the restroom?

Q:  What is the dirtiest object in a public bathroom?

Q:  What are considered the 2 cleanest places in a public bathroom?

Q:  Which stall usually has the fewest germs?

Q:  Which public bathroom usually has the most germs – women's or men's room?

Q:  When was the modern toilet invented?

Q:  What movie was the first to show a flushing toilet?

Q:  When was toilet paper invented?

# Fun Bathroom Hygiene Trivia – Answer Page

**Q: What percentage of men wash their hands after using the restroom?**

A: *Only 75% of men wash their hands after using the restroom!*

**Q: What percentage of women wash their hands after using the restroom?**

A: *90% of women wash their hands after using the restroom.*

**Q: What is the dirtiest object in a public bathroom?**

A: *The floor. It was found to have 2 million bacteria per square inch!*

**Q: What are considered the 2 cleanest places in a public bathroom?**

A: *The door knob and the toilet seat.*

**Q: Which stall usually has the fewer germs?**

A: *The first stall. Since most people seek out the last few stalls for privacy, the first stall is the least frequently used.*

**Q: Which public bathroom usually has the most germs – women's or men's room?**

A: *The women's room was found to harbor twice as much bacteria as the men's.*

**Q: When was the modern toilet invented?**

A: *In 1775, a London watchmaker named Alexander Cummings patented a model similar to today's modern toilet. However, very simple toilets have been used since ancient Babylonian times.*

**Q: What movie was the first to show a flushing toilet?**

A: *Psycho.*

**Q: When was toilet paper invented?**

A: *Toilet paper is believed to be invented in China around the year 850. That is long before the invention of the first toilet.*

# Bathroom Hygiene Activity #5
# "I Can Read Your Mind"

## Instructions:

| | |
|---|---|
| | 1. Give each participant 2 pictures of people demonstrating good and poor bathroom hygiene. |
| | 2. Have participants cut and glue the first picture on a "Bathroom Hygiene Thought Bubble Worksheet." |
| | 3. Instruct participants to begin completing the first "Bathroom Hygiene Thought Bubble Worksheet" by determining if the picture is an example of socially O.K. bathroom hygiene or socially inappropriate bathroom hygiene. |
| | 4. To complete the first "Bathroom Hygiene Thought Bubble Worksheet," encourage participants to list the thoughts and feelings the other person would have, based on the bathroom hygiene of the person in the picture. Have them write their answers in the blank thought bubble provided. You may need to support participants if they are having difficulty. For example, you can write a list of potential thoughts and feelings on the board and have participants select from that list (to add extra difficulty, provide some correct answers and some answers that are incorrect). |
| | 5. To complete the assignment, instruct participants to repeat Steps 2-4 using the second picture. |
| | 6. When everyone is finished, have each participant share the end product with the group. |

## Needed Materials:

☐ Instructional Materials and Supports:

"Bathroom Hygiene Thought Bubble Worksheet" (2 copies per participant)

☐ Pictures of people demonstrating a mix of good and poor bathroom habits. Include pictures of people washing their hands, flushing the toilet, entering a clean bathroom, entering a dirty bathroom, etc. Such pictures can easily be found on the Internet by using searching words such as "hand-washing," "flushing the toilet," "clean bathroom," "gross bathroom," "dirty hands," etc. (2 pictures per participant)

☐ Pencils

☐ Scissors

☐ Glue

☐ Binders

☐ Bathroom Hygiene – Lesson Plan 2

# Bathroom Hygiene Thought Bubble Worksheet

## Instructions:

1. Attach a picture in the designated area.
2. Determine if the person in the picture demonstrates socially O.K. bathroom hygiene or socially inappropriate bathroom hygiene by circling the corresponding answer in the area below.
3. Based on the bathroom hygiene of the person in the picture, list the common thoughts and feelings the other person might have in the blank thought bubble provided.

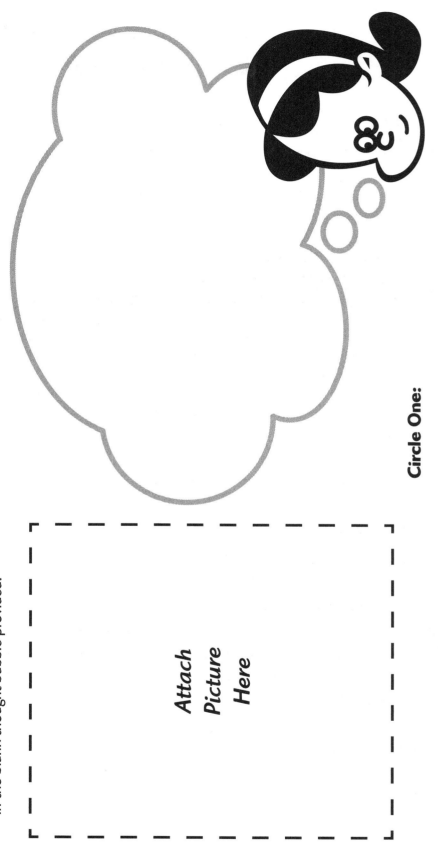

Attach
Picture
Here

**Circle One:**

**Socially O.K. Bathroom Hygiene**

**Socially Inappropriate Bathroom Hygiene**

# Bathroom Hygiene – Lesson Plan 3

## Session Schedule to Post:

- Chat and review
- Fun activity – poster
- Brainstorming session
- Closing (snack, reward, etc.)

## Lesson Details:

| Estimated Time | Activity | Refer to Pages: |
|---|---|---|
| 5 minutes | Opening – Gather participants. Post and review schedule for session | |
| 5 minutes | REVIEW – Have group review the "Bathroom Hygiene Thought Bubble Worksheets" from the previous session | |
| 10 minutes | Bathroom Hygiene Activity #6 – "Bathroom Hygiene Poster" | 165 |
| 20 minutes | Bathroom Hygiene Activity #7 – "The Social Rules of Public Restrooms" | 166-167 |
| 5 minutes | Closing | |

## Needed Materials:

☐ Instructional Materials and Supports:

"The Social Rules of Public Restrooms" (1 copy per participant)

☐ "Bathroom Hygiene Thought Bubble Worksheets" completed during previous lesson

☐ *Optional:* Copies of all completed "Bathroom Hygiene Thought Bubble Worksheets" (allows participants to keep originals in their binders)

☐ Pencils

☐ Scissors

☐ Glue

☐ Markers

☐ Poster board or other large piece of paper (for Bathroom Hygiene Activity #6 – "Bathroom Hygiene Poster")

☐ 1 large piece of paper, divided in half by drawing a line down the center. Label one side "Socially O.K. Behaviors" and the other side, "Socially Inappropriate Behaviors"

☐ Binders

## Following Session, Add to Binder:

☐ "The Social Rules of a Public Restroom" – completed version

# Bathroom Hygiene Activity #6
# "Bathroom Hygiene Poster"

## Instructions:

|   | 1. Gather the completed "Bathroom Hygiene Thought Bubble Worksheets" from Bathroom Hygiene Activity #3 – "I Can Read Your Mind." |
|---|---|
|   | 2. *Optional:* Copy each page so participants can keep originals in their binders. |
|   | 3. Instruct the participants to attach the completed "Bathroom Hygiene Thought Bubble Worksheets" on a poster board or other large piece of paper. |
|   | 4. Display poster in a central area for quick referral. |

## Needed Materials:

☐ Completed "Bathroom Hygiene Thought Bubble Worksheets"

☐ *Optional:* Copies of all completed "Bathroom Hygiene Thought Bubble Worksheets" (allows participants to keep originals in binders)

☐ Markers

☐ Glue

☐ Scissors

☐ Poster board or large piece of paper

☐ Pencils

☐ Binders

☐ Bathroom Hygiene – Lesson Plan 3

# Bathroom Hygiene Activity #7
# "The Social Rules of a Public Restroom"

## Instructions:

|   |   |
|---|---|
|   | 1. Before the start of the activity, position the participants so that everyone can see the large paper (hang on wall for easiest viewing). |
|   | 2. *Optional:* Give each participant a copy of "The Social Rules of a Public Restroom." Instruct participants to follow along with the activity and write the answers in the appropriate sections. |
|   | 3. Introduce the activity using the following discussion questions:<br>• Are there certain behaviors that are considered socially O.K. in a public restroom? How do you determine if something is socially O.K.?<br>• Are there certain behaviors that are considered socially inappropriate in a public restroom? How do you determine if something is socially inappropriate?<br>• Is this list of rules written and posted somewhere? If not, how do so many people "know" the rules?<br>• Is the list of social rules different for the women's bathroom than the men's bathroom? What are some differences? |
|   | 4. Start the brainstorming session by asking participants to list the behaviors that are considered socially O.K. in a public restroom. Write the answers in the designated section on the large paper. If appropriate, determine if the behavior is specific to the women's room vs. the men's room. |
|   | 5. *Optional:* Remind participants to write answers on their worksheets. |
|   | 6. Ask participants to brainstorm behaviors that are considered socially inappropriate in a public restroom. Write the answers in the designated section on the large paper. If appropriate, determine if the behavior is specific to the women's room vs. the men's room. |
|   | 7. Remind participants to write answers on their worksheets. |

## Needed Materials:

☐ Instructional Materials and Supports:

"The Social Rules of a Public Restroom" (1 copy per participant)

☐ Markers

☐ 1 large piece of paper, divided in half by drawing a line down the center. Label one side "Socially O.K. Behaviors" and the other, "Socially Inappropriate Behaviors"

☐ Tape to hang paper

☐ Pencils

☐ Binders

☐ Bathroom Hygiene – Lesson Plan 3

# The Social Rules of a Public Restroom

**Instructions:** Write answers generated from Bathroom Hygiene Activity #7 – "The Social Rules of a Public Restroom" in the spaces provided below.

| Socially O.K. Behaviors | Socially Inappropriate Behaviors |
|---|---|
| 1. | 1. |
| 2. | 2. |
| 3. | 3. |
| 4. | 4. |
| 5. | 5. |
| 6. | 6. |
| 7. | 7. |
| 8. | 8. |

# Bathroom Hygiene – Lesson Plan 4

## Session Schedule to Post:

- Chat and review
- Active game
- Game at table
- Closing (snack, reward, etc.)

## Lesson Details:

| Estimated Time | Activity | Refer to Pages: |
|---|---|---|
| 5 minutes | Opening – Gather participants. Post and review schedule for session | |
| 5 minutes | REVIEW – Review poster on display created during Bathroom Hygiene Activity #7 "The Social Rules of a Public Restroom" from previous lesson plan | |
| 20 minutes | Bathroom Hygiene Activity #8 – "The Urinal Game" | 169-171 |
| 10 minutes | Bathroom Hygiene Activity #9 – "Every Vote Counts" | 172-173 |
| 5 minutes | Closing | |

## Needed Materials:

☐ Instructional Materials and Supports:

"Number Cards for Urinal Game" (1 copy – cut, pasted on firm paper, and laminated)
"Scenario Cards for Urinal Game" (1 copy – cut, pasted on firm paper, and laminated)
"Bathroom Behavior Voting Cards 1" (1 "Socially O.K. Bathroom Behavior Card" and 1 "Socially Inappropriate Bathroom Behavior Card" per participant)

☐ Easy view of poster created during Bathroom Hygiene Activity #7 – "The Social Rules of a Public Restroom" from previous lesson plan

☐ Paper for scorekeeping

☐ Tape for securing number cards

☐ 10-15 pictures of people demonstrating socially O.K. or socially inappropriate bathroom behaviors. These pictures can easily be found on the Internet by search using words such as "hand-washing," "flushing the toilet," "using the urinal," "using a public bathroom," "dirty hands," etc. Cut and paste pictures on construction paper or other firm paper. Laminate, if desired

☐ Prize for winner(s) of Bathroom Hygiene Activity #9 – "Every Vote Counts"

☐ Pencils

☐ Binders

## Following Session, Add to Binder:

Not applicable

# Bathroom Hygiene Activity #8
# "The Urinal Game"

## Instructions:

| | | |
|---|---|---|
| | 1. | Before the start of the game, lay each of the "Number Cards for Urinal Game" in order on the floor in a single file. This is to mimic the line of urinals in a public restroom. |
| | 2. | Read the first scenario from the "Scenario Cards for Urinal Game" to participants. *Optional:* Place an object or another participant on each "urinal" that is occupied in scenario. |
| | 3. | Based on the scenario, instruct the first participant to walk over to the line of numbers and stand on the number (or "urinal") that indicates the most socially O.K. urinal to use. |
| | 4. | Ask the participant to explain why he chose that number (or "urinal"). Also, have him guess what the other person(s) in the scenario would think of him based on the "urinal" selected. |
| | 5. | Award the participant points. A total of 3 points per turn may be earned.<br>    1 point = choosing appropriate "urinal"<br>    1 point = accurate rationale for choice<br>    1 point = accurate guess of what others are thinking |
| | 6. | Repeat Steps 2-4, giving each participant a turn until all scenario cards have been used. |
| | 7. | The participant who scores the most points wins. |

## Needed Materials:

☐ Instructional Materials and Supports:

"Number Cards for Urinal Game" (1 copy – cut, pasted on firm paper, and laminated)

☐ "Scenario Cards for Urinal Game" (1 copy – cut, pasted on firm paper, and laminated)

☐ Marker

☐ Paper for scorekeeping

☐ Binders

☐ Bathroom Hygiene – Lesson Plan 4

# Number Cards for Urinal Game

**Leader's Instructions:** Cut and paste each number on a piece of construction paper or other firm paper. Laminate, if desired. Use for Bathroom Hygiene Activity #8 – "The Urinal Game."

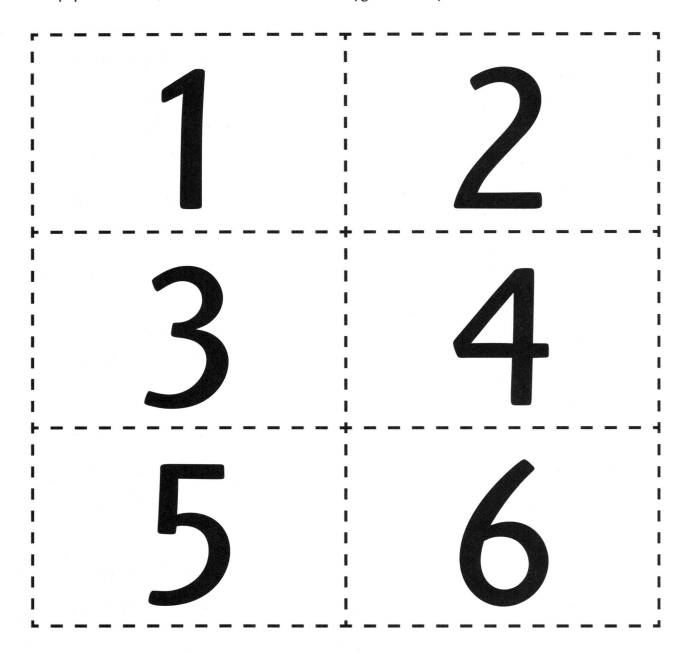

# Scenario Cards for Urinal Game

**Leader's Instructions:** Cut and paste each statement on an index card. Laminate, if desired. Use for Bathroom Hygiene Activity #8 – "The Urinal Game."

| | |
|---|---|
| There are 6 urinals. Urinal 1 *is* occupied. | There are 6 urinals. Urinal 1 and 3 are occupied. |
| There are 6 urinals. Urinals 1 and 6 are occupied. | There are 6 urinals. Urinal 6 is occupied. |
| There are 6 urinals. Urinals 2 and 4 are occupied. | There are 6 urinals. None are occupied. |
| There are 6 urinals. Urinals 2, 4, and 6 are occupied. | There are 6 urinals. Urinals 5 and 6 are occupied. |
| There are 3 urinals. Urinal 1 is occupied. | There are 3 urinals. None are occupied. |

# Bathroom Hygiene Activity #9
# "Every Vote Counts"

## Instructions:

|   |   |
|---|---|
|   | 1. At the start of the game, give each participant 2 Bathroom Behavior Voting Cards: 1 "Socially O.K. Bathroom Behavior Card" and 1 "Socially Inappropriate Bathroom Behavior Card." |
|   | 2. Explain directions of game. |
|   | 3. Show a picture of a person demonstrating either an appropriate bathroom behavior or an inappropriate bathroom behavior. |
|   | 4. Have participants vote by raising the card that represents the bathroom behavior of the person in the picture. |
|   | 5. The first participant to have the correct answer in the air wins 1 point. |
|   | 6. Repeat Steps 3-5 to continue the game, keeping track of each participant's points. |
|   | 7. At the conclusion of the game, award prizes to the high-point earners. |

## Needed Materials:

☐ Instructional Materials and Supports:

"Bathroom Behavior Voting Cards 1" (1 "Socially O.K. Bathroom Behavior Card" and 1 "Socially Inappropriate Bathroom Behavior Card" per participant)

☐ 10-15 pictures of people demonstrating good or poor bathroom behaviors. Such pictures can easily be found on the Internet by using search words such as "hand-washing," "flushing the toilet," "using the urinal," "using a public bathroom," "dirty hands," etc. Cut and paste pictures on construction paper or other firm paper. Laminate, if desired

☐ Pencils

☐ Binders

☐ Bathroom Hygiene – Lesson Plan 4

# Bathroom Behavior Voting Cards 1

**Leader's Instructions:** Cut out each card following the bold line. Glue onto construction paper or other firm paper. Laminate cards. Use for Bathroom Hygiene Activity #9 – "Every Vote Counts."

# Bathroom Hygiene – Lesson Plan 5

## Session Schedule to Post:

- Chat and review
- Game
- Wrap-up game
- Closing (snack, reward, etc.)

## Lesson Details:

| Estimated Time | Activity | Refer to Pages: |
|---|---|---|
| 5 minutes | Opening – Gather participants. Post and review schedule for session | |
| 5 minutes | REVIEW – Encourage participants to recall Bathroom Hygiene Activity #9 – "Every Vote Counts." Review the unwritten social rules surrounding this topic | |
| 20 minutes | Bathroom Hygiene Activity #10 – "Reaction Time" | 175-177 |
| 10 minutes | Bathroom Hygiene Activity #11 – "Bathroom Hygiene Wrap-Up" | 178-179 |
| 5 minutes | Closing | |

## Needed Materials:

☐ Instructional Materials and Supports:

"Bathroom Behavior Voting Cards 2" (1 "Socially O.K. Bathroom Behavior Card" and 1 "Socially Inappropriate Bathroom Behavior Card" per participant)

"Reaction Time Game Cards – Bathroom Behavior" (1 copy – cut, glued on firm paper, and laminated)

"Bathroom Hygiene Wrap-Up Questions" (1 copy – cut, glued on firm paper, and laminated)

☐ Grand prize for Bathroom Hygiene Activity #11 – "Bathroom Hygiene Wrap-Up" (1 per participant)

☐ Pencils

☐ Binders

## Following Session, Add to Binder:

Not applicable

# Bathroom Hygiene Activity #10
## "Reaction Time"

## Instructions:

| | |
|---|---|
| 1. | Prior to the start of the game, place all game cards face down on table. |
| 2. | Pass out the "Bathroom Behavior Voting Cards 2." Each participant should have 1 "Socially O.K. Bathroom Behavior Card" and 1 "Socially Inappropriate Bathroom Behavior Card." |
| 3. | Instruct the first participant to select one game card and read it aloud to the group. Then, the participant must either role-play or verbally describe the action she would take in the given situation. Encourage the participant to explain why she would take that action. Ensure that the participants are choosing socially appropriate solutions and that they are connecting these solutions to the thoughts and feelings of other people. |
| 4. | Using the voting cards, have the remaining participants vote on the participant's solution, determining if it is a socially O.K. or socially inappropriate action. Ask the remaining participants to explain their votes. |
| 5. | Repeat Steps 3-4, switching participants, until all game cards have been used. |

## Needed Materials:

☐ Instructional Materials and Supports:

"Bathroom Behavior Voting Cards 2" (1 "Socially O.K. Bathroom Behavior Card" and 1 "Socially Inappropriate Bathroom Behavior Card" per participant)

"Reaction Time Game Cards – Dealing with Bathroom Behaviors" (1 copy – cut, glued on firm paper, and laminated)

☐ Pencils

☐ Binders

☐ Bathroom Hygiene – Lesson Plan 5

# Bathroom Behavior Voting Cards 2

**Leader's Instructions:** Cut out each card following the bold line. Glue onto construction paper or other firm paper. Laminate cards. Use for Bathroom Hygiene Activity #10 – "Reaction Time."

# Reaction Time Game Cards – Bathroom Behaviors

**Leader's Instructions:** Copy this page. Cut cards on the dotted line. Paste on construction paper or other firm paper and laminate (optional). Use cards to play Bathroom Hygiene Activity #10 – "Reaction Time."

| | |
|---|---|
| You walk into a public bathroom and all of the stalls/urinals are occupied. | You are using the toilet/urinal in a public restroom and a stranger starts to talk to you. |
| You are in a public bathroom and your stomach really hurts. Should you make noise? | You are in a public bathroom and a stranger walks out without washing his hands. |
| You are waiting for a stall to free up and a stranger finally is finished and frees up a stall. You enter the stall and discover that she did not flush the toilet. | You walk into an empty public bathroom and enter a stall. The toilet was not flushed. |
| The stranger at the urinal next to you keeps looking over at you. | After using the toilet, you discover that your stall is out of toilet paper. There are people in the stalls next to you. |
| You are in a public restroom and a stranger in the next stall farts really loud. | You come out of a stall and all of the sinks are in use. |

# Bathroom Hygiene Activity #11
# "Bathroom Hygiene Wrap-Up"

## Instructions:

| | | |
|---|---|---|
| | 1. | Before the start of the game, spread cards face down on table. |
| | 2. | Explain to participants that the objective of the game is for them earn at least 6 points. If the participant or the group of participants earns at least 6 points collectively, they earn a grand prize. |
| | 3. | To start game, have a participant choose a card and read it out loud. |
| | 4. | Encourage participant to answer the question as thoroughly and accurately as possible. |
| | 5. | Award 1 point if answered correctly. |
| | 6. | Repeat Steps 3-5 until all cards have been used. |
| | 7. | Pass out grand prize if participant or group of participants earned 6 points. |

## Needed Materials:

☐ Instructional Materials and Supports:

"Bathroom Hygiene Wrap-Up Questions" (1 copy – cut, pasted on firm paper, and laminated)

☐ Grand prizes

☐ Pencils

☐ Binders

# Bathroom Hygiene Wrap-Up Questions

**Leader's Instructions:** Cut out each question and glue onto construction paper or other firm paper. Laminate cards. Use for Bathroom Hygiene Activity #11 – "Bathroom Hygiene Wrap-Up."

1. What does bathroom hygiene mean?

2. Why is bathroom hygiene important?

3. What do you think about someone with good bathroom hygiene?

4. What do you think about someone with poor bathroom hygiene?

5. What do others think of you when you have good bathroom hygiene?

6. What do others think of you when you have poor bathroom hygiene?

7. What do you need to do in the bathroom to have good bathroom hygiene?

8. What are some of the social rules in a public restroom?

# Chapter 7

# Conclusion

Many factors can lead to poor hygiene in individuals with ASD. Frequently, issues such as sensory sensitivities are addressed, but the hygiene difficulties remain. This is often because the significant impact of impaired perspective-taking skills on hygiene is overlooked. Many individuals with ASD have impaired perspective taking that directly impacts their ability to acquire and maintain socially appropriate hygiene and related behaviors. For example, they do not naturally link personal hygiene habits to their ability to make a good impression on others. When working on hygiene skills with these individuals, it is important, therefore, to teach both *how* to have good hygiene and *why* it is important, and to do so in a concrete and meaningful manner.

*Hygiene and Related Behaviors for Children and Adolescents with Autism Spectrum and Related Disorders* provides an avenue to teach crucial hygiene skills and associated perspective-taking concepts in a fun, yet structured and meaningful manner. Remember, the goal is to laugh and have fun while improving very important life skills. Enjoy!

# References and Resources

# References

Attwood, T. (2004). *Exploring feelings: Cognitive behavior therapy to manage anxiety.* Arlington, TX: Future Horizons.

Attwood, T. (2004). *Exploring feelings: Cognitive behavior therapy to manage anger.* Arlington, TX: Future Horizons.

Attwood, T. (2007). *The complete guide to Asperger's Syndrome.* Philadelphia: Jessica Kingsley Publishing.

Baron-Cohen, S., Leslie, A .M., & Frith, U. (1985). Does the autistic child have a "theory of mind"? *Cognition, 2,* 37-46.

Bellini, S. (2006). *Building social relationships: A systematic approach to teaching social interaction skills to children and adolescents with autism spectrum disorders and other social difficulties.* Shawnee Mission, KS: Autism Asperger Publishing Company.

Buron, K. D., & Curtis, M. (2003). *The incredible 5-point scale.* Shawnee Mission, KS: Autism Asperger Publishing Company.

Buron, K. D. (2007). *A "5" could make me lose control.* Shawnee Mission, KS: Autism Asperger Publishing Company.

Gray, C. (1994). *Comic strip conversations.* Arlington, TX: Future Horizons.

Kerstein, L. (2008). *My sensory book: Working together to explore sensory issues and the big feelings they can cause: A workbook for parents, professionals, and children.* Shawnee Mission, KS: Autism Asperger Publishing Company.

Myles, B. S., & Southwick, J. (2005). *Asperger Syndrome and difficult moments: Practical Solutions for tantrums, rage, and meltdowns* (rev. ed.). Shawnee Mission, KS: Autism Asperger Publishing.

Myles, B. S., Trautman, M. L., & Schelvan, R. L. (2004). *The hidden curriculum: Practical solutions for understanding unstated rules in social situations.* Shawnee Mission, KS: Autism Asperger Publishing Company.

Winner, M. (2002). *Thinking about you: Thinking about me.* San Jose, CA: Think Social Publishing, Inc.

Winner, M. (2005). *Think social! A social thinking curriculum for school-age students.* San Jose, CA: Think Social Publishing, Inc.

Williams, M. S., & Shellenberger, S. (1994). *How does your engine run? A leader's guide to the Alert Program for self-regulation.* Albuquerque, NM: Therapy Works.

# Resources

# Tips for Finding Pictures

The Internet is an excellent resource and contains many, many entertaining pictures that can support the activities in this curriculum. There are many ways to locate pictures. Here are a few suggestions:

1.  Go to a main search engine such as:

    www.google.com

    www.yahoo.com

    www.msn.com

2.  Click on "Images"

3.  In the search bar enter terms such as the following:
    *   Poor Hygiene
    *   Dirty Nails
    *   Nail Fungus
    *   Dirty Hair
    *   Gross Hair
    *   Dirty Teeth
    *   Gross Teeth
    *   Tooth Decay
    *   Unkempt
    *   Nice Smile
    *   Healthy Teeth
    *   Healthy
    *   Clean Nails
    *   Clean Hair
    *   Picking Nose
    *   Picking Teeth
    *   Dental Floss
    *   Food in Teeth
    *   Blowing Nose

# Tips Regarding Movie Clips

The Internet is an excellent resource and contains many, many entertaining video/movie clips that can support the activities in this curriculum. There are many ways to locate clips. Here are some suggestions:

1. Go to a website such as:

   www.google.com

   www.yahoo.com

   www.msn.com

   www.youtube.com

2. Click on "Video(s)"

3. In the search bar enter the terms such as the following:

   - Farting
   - Burping
   - Public Bathroom
   - Social Norms in Restroom
   - Bathroom Etiquette

   - Also, several movies contain clips surrounding topics in this curriculum. Here are some examples:
     1. Along Came Polly (2 clips of bathroom behaviors)
     2. Daddy Day Care (clip of bathroom behaviors)
     3. Elf (clip of burping)

# Helpful Websites

## General Hygiene

- http://kidshealth.org – KidsHealth is a large site providing doctor-approved health information about children from before birth through adolescence. It contains great information about hygiene and related issues.

- http://www.cyh.com – This website, sponsored by Children and Youth Health in Southern Australia, provides health information for kids, teens and young adults.

- http://www.pgschoolprograms.com – This website provides lesson plans, worksheets, videos and other materials for teaching topics such as oral care, puberty and nutrition.

## Oral Hygiene

- www.oralb.com – This website contains helpful information about oral hygiene, including articles on how to make oral hygiene fun for kids.

- www.crest.com – This website, under the "Crest Kids" section, contains helpful information about oral hygiene for kids.

- http://www.ada.org/public/education/teachers/smilesmarts – The American Dental Association (ADA) provides a oral health curriculum for ages 4-14 years that is free to download.

## Farts and Burps

- http://www.fartifacts.com – This website contains many facts, video clips, and links related to flatulence.

- http://www.heptune.com/farts.html – This website provides a comprehensive list of facts related to farts.

# APC

Autism Asperger Publishing Co.
P.O. Box 23173
Shawnee Mission, Kansas 66283-0173
www.asperger.net • 913-897-1004